2005

RESILIENCE

— ◆ —

RESILIENCE

— ◆ —

Rebounding When Life's Upsets
Knock You Down

H. Norman Wright

14022

SERVANT PUBLICATIONS
ANN ARBOR, MICHIGAN

Vine Books is an imprint of Servant Publications especially designed to serve evangelical Christians.

Some of the stories that appear in this book are true and have been freely shared with the author and used by permission of the individuals involved. Other stories have been drawn from the author's counseling and personal experiences as fictional composites. Any similarity between the names and characterizations and real people is unintended and purely coincidental.

Unless otherwise credited, Scripture quotations are from the New American Standard Bible © The Lockman Foundation 1960, 1962, 1963, 1968, 1971, 1972, 1973, 1975, 1977. NIV indicates those Scriptures that are taken from the HOLY BIBLE, NEW INTERNATIONAL VERSION®. © 1973, 1978, 1984 by International Bible Society. Used by permission of Zondervan Publishing House. All rights reserved. Verses marked AMP are from the Amplified Bible. Old Testament ©1965, 1987, by the Zondervan Corporation. The Amplified New Testament © 1958, 1987 by the Lockman Foundation. Used by permission. Scripture quotations marked NKJV are from the New King James Version, © 1979, 1980, 1982, Thomas Nelson Inc., Publishers. Verses marked RSV are from the Revised Standard Version of the Bible, © 1946, 1952, 1971 by the Division of Christian Education of the National Council of Churches of Christ in the USA. Used by permission. Verses marked LB are from *The Living Bible*, ©1971 owned by assignment by KNT Charitable Trust. All rights reserved.

Published by Servant Publications
P.O. Box 8617
Ann Arbor, Michigan 48107

97 98 9 9 00 10 9 8 7 6 5 4 3 2 1

Printed in the United States of America
ISBN 0-89283-939-2

LIBRARY OF CONGRESS CATALOGING-IN-PUBLICATION DATA

Wright, H. Norman
Resilience : rebounding when life's upsets knock you down / H. Norman Wright.
    p.   cm.
 ISBN 0-89283-939-2
1. Consolation.   2. Suffering—Religious aspects—Christianity.   3. Life change events—Religious aspects—Christianity.   4. Resilience (Personality trait)—Religious aspects—Christianity.   I. Title.
BV4905.2.W753   1997
248.8'6—dc21   97-3296
                                                                        CIP

CONTENTS

— ◆ —

ONE

— ◆ —

"Why Did This Happen to Me?"

Understanding the Meaning of Crisis

All eyes were glued to the young man who stood poised just two inches from the edge of a platform over two hundred feet in the air. From his perspective the distance probably seemed as deep as the abyss of the Grand Canyon. The people on the ground looked on with quiet fascination, waiting, just waiting. The man lifted one foot a few inches in the air, hesitated and put it back down. Then he took a deep breath, blinked his eyes and stepped out into space. Down and down he fell until his tether stretched taut. All of a sudden he seemed to rocket back up toward the platform. The elasticity of the bungee line shot him skyward. It had resilience. It had the ability to bounce back.

One of the toys I remember from my childhood was a paddle with a long rubber band and a small rubber ball attached to it. You hit the little ball with the paddle as hard as you could to make it fly out as far as possible, stretching the rubber band to its limit. Let me tell you, it had resilience! Sometimes that ball came flying back at me like a missile, and all too frequently it missed the paddle and hit me! I quickly learned to respect the power of elasticity.

Over the years I've discovered that some people have the capability of bouncing back—they have *resilience*. But others don't. Perhaps you've wondered as I have what makes the difference. Why is it that some people have the ability to bounce back after adversity while others do not? That is the purpose of this book—to discover the way not only to survive but to grow through life's problems.

Stories of survival are all around us. The *Reader's Digest* has carried many of them. One *Reader's Digest* told the story of four fishermen from a Central American country. One day as they were out fishing, something happened to their boat. It just wouldn't work anymore. Soon they were caught in the currents and swept out of sight of land and the shipping lanes. The men were adrift for months before they were discovered still alive. The focus of the article was on how they survived.

A newspaper carries the story of a plane crash in the mountains during the heart of winter. The combination of the snowstorms and the rugged terrain prevented the rescuers from getting to the plane for ten days. Fearing the worst, they were amazed to discover fourteen people still alive. One of the first questions the rescuers asked was, "How did you survive?"

Then there are those who experience never ending crises. Perhaps that's where you or someone you love is living right now. Your crisis could take the form of a devastating illness that destroys all the dreams you've been working toward for years. Your finances have been drained and the numbing ache of exhaustion and despair has crept into the life of your family. Perhaps you have a child who has run away from home or chosen a lifestyle totally in opposition to your values. Or what about the family whose eight-year-old girl was struck by a car as she rode her bicycle around a blind corner? This happened twenty years ago, and she still can't speak or move. Twenty years of waiting, hoping, putting their dreams on hold.

How does one survive when over a period of several years two of your adult sons are tragically killed, another son tells you he is gay and your husband has lost his memory of you because of a medical problem? This is not fiction. It happened to Barbara Johnson; you may have read her story. But she's surviving.

A friend of mine who ministered to thousands of young people in a camping ministry over the past twenty years, and who is an outstanding songwriter and singer, can barely walk today. He has difficulty cutting the food on his plate now. His once skilled hands can no longer play the guitar. He has multiple sclerosis. It will never get any better, but he too is surviving.

You probably saw the Superman films with Christopher Reeve playing the title role. He even did some of his own stunts. His life almost ended when his horse stopped at a jump during an equestrian competition. Because his hands were wrapped in the reins, he couldn't put them out to break his fall. He became a "C1-C2," which is the designation for a paralyzing injury between the neck and the brain stem. It's called the "hangman's injury," since the break is the same as that in an execution when the scaffold trapdoor opens and the noose snaps tight. Christopher Reeve went from performing high-risk stunts, skiing, sailing and riding in competitions to being strapped into a wheelchair. He is paralyzed, but he's not only surviving, he has become a spokesperson for all those in similar situations.

I enjoy receiving not just cards at Christmas but also the newsletters telling of the year's events. One friend's letter told of the following experiences: During the past year, nine of her friends at church were diagnosed with cancer and two subsequently died. She and her husband were involved in a head-on collision with another car. Her husband had a kidney stone surgery with complications. His father died later that year. Two friends were sentenced to life in prison, one for poisoning his wife and the other for sexually molesting his granddaughter. Her brother-in-law left his wife and young child for cocaine. Her own brother was suicidal and finally entered an AA program. She was having lunch on an ocean pier with a student from Japan when an elderly man in a wheelchair wheeled himself to the end of the pier near them, lifted himself over the rail and plunged into the ocean in an attempt to kill himself.

You're probably thinking, "That's unbelievable" or "It's too much for one person or family to handle" or "What an overload!" And that's what it was ... overload. But she's surviving.

Your crisis probably doesn't make the news. But it's just as major to you. It hurts just as much. There are so many life-crushing events like the loss of a job, the loss of a spouse through divorce or death, abuse, lawsuit, mental illness in your family, being robbed or victimized in other ways. You know what I'm talking about; you can't help but know. The upsets of life are all around us.

Why is it that some people survive the crises and difficulties of life, yet others don't? Why do some overcome the storms of life while others are overwhelmed by them?

Perhaps it's because we think of storms as exceptions to the rule of calm weather. Maybe our perspective is wrong. I propose that times of calm are more likely the exceptions.

Out of Nowhere and at the Wrong Time

A number of years ago I went fishing on a lake in Minnesota with several relatives. It was a beautiful day. As the afternoon wore on it became very calm and still. Suddenly my cousin said, "Let's head for shore ... quick!" I couldn't believe what I was hearing. The weather was great and the fish were beginning to bite. But my cousin said, "Just wait." By the time we made the shoreline, ten minutes later, we were fighting thirty- to forty-mile-an-hour winds. They seemed to come out of nowhere. For hours we huddled in our tents just waiting for them to be torn from their pegs.

Where did the storm come from? I wondered. One moment the sky was clear, the next we were being buffeted about by strong winds and a torrential rainstorm.

Storms are like that. They often appear out of nowhere at the "wrong time" and are totally inconvenient. They disrupt our plans and some leave devastation in their path. Life is never the same after some storms have swept through our lives.

There are other storms that do give us some warning. They appear gradually and the weather forecasters are able to give us some indication in advance. To some degree we can prepare for these if the predictions are consistent and accurate. But often they aren't, and once again we find ourselves unprepared.

Storms come in all kinds, sizes, shapes and intensities. There are rainstorms, fire storms, hailstorms, snowstorms and windstorms. Nahum the prophet said, "His [the Lord's] way is in the whirlwind and the storm" (1:3b, NIV).

I've been in some storms where the sky was split open by flashing brilliant fingers of lightning followed by ear-deafening thunder. I've stood on the shoreline of Jackson Lake in the Grand Teton National Park and heard the thunder begin to roll through the Teton range twenty miles to the left of me and continue in front of me on up into Yellowstone National Park. It was a breathtaking, awesome experience.

Some storms are so new and different that we aren't sure just what to do when they hit. Southern California is not known for having tornadoes. We have rain, Santa Ana wind conditions, earthquakes, hot weather, but no tornadoes ... until a few years ago when we experienced a full-sized twister on our own street. I wasn't home, but my wife, Joyce, was.

While she was working in the yard she began to feel some strange and strong winds. Realizing that something was wrong, she went inside and shut the door. But the winds continued, and it seemed as though the air was being sucked out of the house by this wind. She didn't know exactly what was happening, so she shut herself in one of the rooms.

About this time a neighbor turned the street corner in time to see the twister touch down in the middle of the block and begin coming toward her. She drove her car into her garage and ran inside the house just before the tornado ripped the large tree from her front yard.

We were fortunate. No homes were lost, but several trees were uprooted. I guess the worst part was that this was trash day, and in front of each home were several full trash cans. After the tornado hit they were all empty! Everyone in our neighborhood was amazed—surprised—stunned. This just doesn't happen in our area. No one knew what to do!

As unpredictable as some weather can be, we can usually tolerate it. But it's the storms of life that throw us.

Crises Are a Normal Part of Life

Do you know what we call some of these storms of life? We call them crises. Some are predictable, some give us a bit of warning, and others penetrate our plans and our lives like the attack of an alien invader. We can't avoid them, *but we can handle them in such a way that they don't cripple or devastate us for the remainder of our lives.*

When we experience a crisis, it seems as though everything is "on the line." Webster defines crisis as a "crucial time" and "a turning point in the course of anything." The term *crisis* is often used to describe a person's internal response to some external hazard. When you or I experience a crisis, at first we are thrown off guard and we temporarily lose our ability to cope. Do you know what I'm talking about? Very possibly you do if you've lived any length of time.

You will be able to handle crises better if you understand what a crisis is and the potential that lies within it for your benefit. Far too often we think of crises as the unusual, mostly negative, events we should avoid when they are actually the stuff of which life is made. Why do I say that? Because crises have the potential for developing Christian character in us.

Sometimes it's difficult to see any potential, any good, any benefit or even any way to recover from a crisis. You can look at the front page of the newspaper or watch the first fifteen minutes of a newscast to see that crises come in all shapes and sizes.

A businessman who lost his business and had to declare bankruptcy had no vision for his future. He wondered if life would ever be stable again. Not only did he repeatedly ask why, he wondered where God was when he needed Him the most. His crisis challenged his beliefs and faith in God. *How could such a loss have any purpose?* he thought. He felt at loose ends, wondering what his first step would be to move forward. The crushing experience immobilized him.

I can think of a more public example. Perhaps you remember a significant day in sports. One of the best hitters for the Montreal Expos was at the plate facing a hard-throwing pitcher for the San Francisco Giants. The pitcher looked at the runner at first base and then threw as hard as he could. Little did he know it was the last pitch he would ever throw in any kind of game. A sharp crack was heard all over the stadium as the bone in Dave Dravecky's arm snapped in two. Those watching saw him grasp his arm; later he said that he'd felt it was going to fly toward home plate. They also heard his scream as he fell to the ground.

It wasn't just that his arm was broken. The doctors found that the cancer he thought was in remission had reappeared. His arm would have to be amputated at the shoulder to ensure the cancer wouldn't spread to the rest of his body.[1]

Can you imagine the questions and thoughts that would run through your mind if you had just gone through this experience? You're losing part of your body. You're losing the skill you've worked for years to perfect. You're probably asking yourself, *What about my identity? What if the cancer spreads? What are my odds of surviving? How will I make a living now?* Numbness, fear and dread soon become your companions.

I think of all the parents of runaway children or teens on drugs. These parents know what a crisis is.

I think of a friend of mine who was driving home from work when he came upon an accident. A car had hit a motorcycle. My friend stopped and went over to the car to see if the occupants were all right. They were. He then walked toward the downed motorcycle and felt a subtle sense of recognition within. As he stepped over the green motorcycle and lifted the visor of the rider's helmet, he recognized the face of his nineteen-year-old son, who was dead. His entire family entered into a crisis.

When you lose a loved one, there's a large aching hole in your life. Your sense of disbelief coupled with the numbness soon evolves to the pain of realizing that the person is dead … gone. My friend felt as though part of him had been cut away when the full reality of his son's death hit him. He thought, *My son will never come through that door again with a smile on his face.* Any future with his son had been destroyed.

I read the personal story of a professor's nightmare as he described it in his book, *A Grace Disguised*:

We returned to our van, loaded and buckled up, and left for home. By then it was dark. Ten minutes into our trip home I noticed an oncoming car on a lonely stretch of highway driving extremely fast. I slowed down at a curve, but the other car did not. It jumped its lane and smashed head-on into our minivan. I learned later that the alleged driver was Native American, drunk, driving eighty-five miles per hour. He was accompanied by his pregnant wife, also drunk, who was killed in the accident.

I remember those first moments after the accident as if everything was happening in slow motion. They are frozen into my memory with a terrible vividness. After recovering my breath, I turned around to survey the damage. The scene was chaotic. I remember the look of terror on the faces of my children and the feeling of horror that swept over me when I saw the unconscious and broken bodies of Lynda, my four-year-old daughter Diana Jane, and my mother. I remember getting Catherine (then eight), David (seven), and John (two) out of the van through my door, the only one that would open. I remember taking pulses, doing mouth-to-mouth resuscitation, trying to save the dying and calm the living. I remember the feeling of panic that struck my soul as I watched Lynda, my mother, and Diana Jane all die before my eyes. I remember the pandemonium that followed: people gawking, lights flashing from emergency vehicles, a helicopter whirring overhead, cars lining up, medical experts doing what they could to help. And I remember the realization sweeping over me that I would soon plunge into a darkness from which I might never again emerge as a sane, normal, believing man.

In the hours that followed the accident, the initial shock gave way to an unspeakable agony. I felt dizzy with grief's vertigo, cut off from family and friends, tormented by the loss, nauseous from the pain. After arriving at the hospital, I paced the floor like a caged animal, only recently captured. I was so bewildered that I was unable to voice questions or think rationally. I felt wild with fear and agitation, as if I was being stalked by some deranged killer from whom I could not escape. I could not stop crying. I could not silence the deafening noise of crunching metal, screaming sirens, and wailing children. I could not rid my eyes of the vision of violence, of shattering glass and shattered bodies. All I wanted was to be dead. Only the sense of responsibility for my three surviving children and the habit of living for forty years kept me alive.[2]

This was a crisis. Part of this man's life had been amputated. Any time we lose something tangible, we also lose something intangible but just as real.

Crisis Kills Our Dreams

With most crises come another unwelcome guest—the death of a dream. Perhaps one of the best expressions of what we experience when this happens comes from the poet Langston Hughes:

> ... if dreams die
> life is a broken-winged bird
> that cannot fly.
> ... when dreams go
> life is a barren field
> frozen with snow.[3]

I'm sure Sue felt all the emotion inherent in this poem when something happened to devastate her life. Sue was a woman who had a threefold dream: being a wife, a mother and a missionary. She achieved all three. It seemed as though all her dreams were coming true. She had a husband, two girls and was serving on a foreign mission field. One day she discovered her husband had been involved in an affair. Now she lives in the States, works as a nurse and is rearing her girls alone. She tells about the death of her dream:

There were actually two dreams that died when my husband walked out. One of them was the death of a marriage. I had this vision that I was going to be married for the rest of my life. Now that vision was gone. For a long time I had a mental picture that I was standing at a grave, trying to bury my marriage. The hole was dug, but boards were across the grave so they couldn't put the casket down into the ground. The casket was open and they couldn't continue the burial because I refused to throw in my flowers. I was holding a dead wedding bouquet, my symbol of my marriage. I hung on to that bouquet for a long time.

I knew I was beginning to heal when the day came in my vision that I wanted to pick up some fresh pink carnations for myself and throw the dead bouquet into the casket. That's when I knew I was beginning to let go of my grief.[4]

Building New Dreams

We need to grieve over destroyed dreams. But there's something else that can happen to a dream. When it doesn't die, yet it gets damaged, the dream is altered. Then you have to begin building your dream anew.

I dreamed that my daughter would attend college. After all, I had almost nine years of college and graduate school behind me! I learned there was another reason I had such high expectations for Sheryl. Our son, Matthew, was profoundly retarded and would never be more than an infant mentally. This added to my desire that Sheryl go to college. Plus, I taught at a Christian university at the time and her tuition would be free.

After one year of college Sheryl said it wasn't for her. After half of a semester at fashion design school she dropped out and said she was going to cosmetology school to become a manicurist. Our initial dream was damaged and we wondered where this new dream would lead. Little did we know what would happen!

Today Sheryl is one of the leading nail technicians and nail artists in the nation! She has won most of the national and international nail competitions. She owns her own salon, has published her own nail art book and is asked to teach and judge events all over the country. She has reached *her* dreams. Our dreams needed to be altered to line up with hers. There are times when we all need to accept altered dreams in order to move ahead.

Throughout your city or town right now, many people are experiencing their own world-collapsing crises:

- A young man's heart, which had become a receptacle of love for a certain young lady, is now filled with pain he could never have imagined because she said no to his marriage proposal.

- A family has had no income for months. The unemployment checks have run out and there are no prospects at all for a job.

- A young athlete who has spent fifteen years working toward his dream of playing professional ball hears the surgeon say, "Your knee injury is beyond repair."

- A young mother who has gone to check on her three-month-old baby finds that he's a victim of SIDS (Sudden Infant Death Syndrome).

- The forty-year-old man who has just walked out of his doctor's office in a dazed fog is still trying to make sense of the deadly prognosis he's just heard.

The crises you and I experience can be the result of one event or of several. The crisis may be great or overwhelming, such as the death of a child, or it could be a problem that has a special significance just for you that makes it overwhelming. The crisis could be a problem that comes at a time of special vulnerability or when you're unprepared. I'm sure you've had to handle a stopped-up sink. Usually this presents no real difficulty except for the inconvenience. But if the sink stops up when you've had the flu and little or no sleep for two nights, you feel overwhelmed. It's the last straw!

If a problem occurs when your coping abilities are not functioning well, or when you don't have the support or help from others that you need, you feel overwhelmed and see the event as a crisis.

There are three possible outcomes of a crisis: a change for the better, a change for the worse, or a return to the previous level of functioning. The word *crisis* is rich with meaning. The Chinese term for *crisis (weiji)* is made up of two symbols: one is for danger and the other for opportunity. The English word is based on the Greek word *(krinein),* meaning "to decide." Crisis is a time of decision and judgment, as well as a turning point during which there will be a change for the better or worse.

When a doctor talks about a crisis, he is talking about the moment in the course of a disease when a change for the better or worse occurs. When a counselor talks about a marital crisis, he or she is talking about the turning point when the marriage can go in either direction; it can move toward growth, enrichment and improvement, or it can move toward dissatisfaction, pain and, in some cases, dissolution. As you think of the crises you've experienced, how did they turn out? A change for the better, for the worse or back to normal?

Crisis is not always bad; it can become a turning point in your life for the better. Yes, it can bring danger and upset, but it also carries with it opportunity for growth and change. As you try to discover a way to cope with crisis, you could discover a new and better way of living.

TWO

— ◆ —

"Get Me Out of This"

Coping with the Inevitability of Crisis

Crisis. What is it specifically? How do you know when you're in crisis?

Four elements work together to make up that state of being. When you are aware of the four elements and understand how they contribute to the crisis state, you take the first step toward handling life's crises in a more positive manner.

The first element is *a sudden upsetting event*. This can be anything that starts a chain reaction of events, which in turn leads to crisis. For example,

- A young wife who prepared for her career for seven years now discovers she is unexpectedly pregnant.
- A college senior who gave himself to basketball during school in order to play in the professional basketball association shatters an ankle while hiking.
- A widower who is raising five preadolescent children loses his job in a very specialized profession.

What these people have in common is an event that upsets their goals or livelihood.

Whenever you find yourself getting upset or having difficulty coping, ask yourself, "What event is occurring or has just occurred in my life?" The cause of your upset is usually fairly obvious.

The second element contributing to a crisis is *your vulnerability*. Not all negative events lead to crisis. You have to be vulnerable in some way for a crisis to occur. For example, if you go without sleep for a couple of nights, you could be vulnerable to a situation you usually handle without difficulty. Illness or depression lowers a person's coping ability, as do unresolved emotional issues from the past.

Recently, I talked with a woman who wanted to give up her foster child, cancel an important fund-raising event and quit her business. Why? Because she was depressed over the threat of another loss in her life. She was overwhelmed and felt like giving up everything! I asked her not to make any life-changing decisions during her time of depression because she might regret those decisions later on.

The third element in a crisis is *the actual precipitating factor.* You know, the last straw! These are the times when you seem to cope with one upsetting event after another, then go to pieces when you drop a piece of food on your clothes. In reality, your reaction to dropping the food is a reaction to all of the other events. It's like saving up all of your upsets and dumping the whole load when a family member does something you don't like. Out comes all the accumulated anger at once. Most, if not all, of the anger is about things completely unrelated to what your family member just did.

The last element is *the state of crisis.* Everyone differs in the way they handle a crisis. If I were to ask how you respond to crisis, what would you say? When you feel that you can no longer handle what is happening in your life, then it becomes a crisis. There are several indications of this state.

Usually there are actual symptoms of stress, which include physiological or psychological factors, or both. These symptoms can include depression, anxiety, headaches, bleeding ulcers and more. In other words, you experience some type of extreme discomfort.

You also experience a sense of panic or defeat. You may feel as though you've tried everything, and nothing works. You feel like a failure; you feel defeated, overwhelmed, helpless. Hope? There is no hope.

At this point you can respond in one of two ways: one way is to become agitated and engage in behavior that is actually counterproductive—pacing back and forth, taking drugs, driving too fast, getting into arguments or fights. The other response is to become apathetic and is equally counterproductive. This could include excessive sleeping or drinking to the extent that you no longer feel the pain.

Your main concern at this point is getting relief. *"Get me out of this!"* We want relief from the pain of the stress. And we want it now. Instead, we wait—for others, for relief, for God to respond to our prayers and change our situation.

In a major crisis we are not usually in a condition to solve our problems in a rational manner. This adds to our state of confusion, since we're usually capable of functioning quite well. Shock makes a person appear dazed and respond in bizarre ways. If you're in shock, you may feel frantic and look to other people for help. In fact, you may become very dependent upon others to help you out of the dilemma.

This is also a time of decreased efficiency. You may continue to function normally, but instead of responding at 100 percent capacity, your response may be at 60 percent. This, too, disturbs you. The greater the threat from our own appraisal of what's happening, the less ability we will have to cope.

To Be or Not to Be a Crisis

Is it possible to avoid experiencing a crisis? Not really, for crises are a part of life. Some situations are true crises; others are problems that escalate into crisis.

There are three factors that affect the intensity of a crisis and may even contribute to an event becoming a crisis. They are how you view a problem, how much support you have from others and how strong are your coping mechanisms.

First let's talk about the way you view a problem and the meaning it has for you. Some events would be threatening for anyone, whereas some would be threatening *just for you*. Sometimes your perception makes the event threatening. Your beliefs, ideas, expectations and perceptions all work together as you determine whether or not a situation is a crisis.

We all have our own way of perceiving an event. If a friend responds to a certain event more intensely than you do, the event probably has more meaning for your friend than it does for you.

Two people can view the same event differently, depending on several factors. For instance, you appraise the death of a close friend from several viewpoints: how close the relationship was, how often you were in touch with that friend, how you have responded to other losses and how many losses you have experienced recently. A woman deeply involved in her husband's life perceives his death differently than does a close friend, a business associate or the uncle who saw the deceased once every five years.

When you experience a crisis, you are perceiving the loss or threatened loss of something important to you. Think of what is most important to you. Is there anything in your life right now in danger of turning into a crisis? If you're having trouble formulating an answer, perhaps the following scenario can help you discover what is most important to you in your home life:

You've been informed that your house is going to be completely destroyed in ten minutes. You have time to make two trips out of your home, taking with you what is most important and valuable to you. What will you take?

People are often surprised at what has meaning for them and what doesn't. This exercise also causes some people to reevaluate what they feel is important. Consider another scenario:

What one event, were it to occur in the next twelve months, would be the most upsetting or devastating to you? List the next four events in order of importance, using the same criteria. Now think about how you would handle those events and work through the loss involved in each one.

Did you know that even a job promotion can precipitate a crisis? Take Ralph, for example. Ralph was a car salesman promoted to sales manager. This gave him more status, more money and more changes in his relationships. He no longer was on the same level as the other salesmen and now had to push and urge them to make their sales quotas. He was quite uncomfortable in this role and became so dissatisfied that he began to call in sick to avoid the pressure and conflicts. His loss of confidence threw him into a crisis.

A second factor that affects the intensity of a crisis is whether or not we have an adequate network of friends, relatives or agencies to support us. This is where the body of Christ should come into play as one of the greatest support groups available. But the church needs to know how to respond at such a time. I know of several churches that respond to a person or family's loss of a loved one by having a different family assigned to minister to them each week for a year. They call the family, send notes, deliver food, take them out and so on.

A third factor that helps determine whether an event becomes a crisis or not involves a person's coping mechanisms. If your coping mechanisms do not function well, or they break down quickly, then crisis is inevitable. Some coping mechanisms are healthy, while others are destructive. Coping mechanisms run the gamut—rationalization, denial, researching what others say, praying, reading Scripture and more. The greater the number and diversity of *healthy* coping methods a person employs, the less likely it is that a problem or upset will become a crisis.

Typical Responses to Crisis

When you experience a crisis, your response may differ from that of family members or friends. However, there are some basic responses common to all people, depending on what comforts them during difficult times. Take a look at some typical responses and see if you can identify how you respond to crisis.

- Some individuals look for others to protect and control them at a time of crisis. They say, "Please take over for me."
- Some need a person who will help them maintain contact with what is real and what isn't. They say, "Help me know that I am real at this time. Help me know what is going on right now."
- Some feel terribly empty and need loving contact with others. They say, "Care for me; love me."

- Some need another person to be available at all times in order to feel secure. They say, "Always be there. Never leave."
- Some have an urgent need to talk. They say, "Let me get this off my chest. Listen to me again and again."
- Some need advice on certain pressing matters. They say, "Tell me what to do."
- Some need to sort out their conflicting thoughts. They say, "Help me put things into perspective."
- Some need the assistance of some type of specialist. They say, "I need some professional advice."

Perhaps you identify with some of these responses. If so, why not share your need with those closest to you? When crisis hits it will help you feel more in control and keep you from feeling overwhelmed.

Those Who Flounder

Why do some people seem to handle crisis well, while others don't? Let's consider some characteristics of those who appear to have the most difficulty handling a crisis.

Some individuals are *emotionally fragile* to begin with, and specific events are more difficult for them to handle.

Those who have a *physical ailment or illness* will struggle because they have fewer resources upon which to draw.

Those who *deny reality* have a hard time coping with a crisis. Some may deny the fact that they are seriously ill or financially ruined or that their child is on drugs or has a terminal illness.

Dr. Ralph Hirschowitz, a Harvard psychiatrist, has created a term for the next characteristic. He calls it "magic of the mouth," which is the tendency to eat, drink, smoke and talk excessively. When crisis enters these people's lives, they seem to regress into self-medication through their mouths. They feel uncomfortable unless they're doing something with their mouths most of the time, such as eating, talking, smoking. This *refusal to face the real problem* can continue after the crisis is over and can actually help to create an additional crisis for the person.

Another characteristic is an *unrealistic approach to time*. Some people crowd the time dimensions of a problem or they extend the time factors way into the future. They want the problem to be "fixed" right away, or they delay addressing it. Delay avoids the discomfort of reality but enlarges the problem.

People who struggle with *excessive guilt* will have difficulty coping with a crisis. They tend to blame themselves for the difficulty, which increases feelings of guilt, which further immobilizes them.

People who place blame have a difficult time coping with a crisis. They do not focus on what the problem is, they *focus on "who caused the problem."* Their approach is to find enemies, either real or imagined, and project blame on them.

Another characteristic of those who do not cope well with crisis is the tendency to be *overly dependent or overly independent*. Such people either turn away from offers of help or become clinging vines. Those who cling tend to suffocate you if you're involved in helping them. Overly independent people shun offers of help. They do not cry out for help, even if they're sliding down the hill toward disaster. When the disaster hits they either continue to deny it or blame others for its occurrence.

One other characteristic has a bearing upon all the others—*how a person perceives God*.

Where Is God During a Crisis?

Our belief in God and how we perceive God is a reflection of our theology and will affect how we cope with crisis. Our lives are based upon our theology, yet so many people are frightened by it.

Many times when we go through difficult upsets and crises we are forced to reevaluate what we truly believe. Unfortunately, many people determine what they believe by what they are going through. They allow their theology to be determined by their circumstances. When they hit the problems of life, they seem to negate the promises of God and begin to wonder if He cares!

Sometimes crisis changes our view of God. Max Lucado describes the process well:

There is a window in your heart through which you can see God. Once upon a time that window was clear. Your view of God was crisp. You could see God as vividly as you could see a gentle valley or hillside. The glass was clean, the pane unbroken.

You knew God. You knew how he worked. You knew what he wanted you to do. No surprises. Nothing unexpected. You knew that God had a will, and you continually discovered what it was.

Then, suddenly, the window cracked. A pebble broke the window. A pebble of pain.

Perhaps the stone struck when you were a child and a parent left home—forever. Maybe the rock hit in adolescence when your heart was broken. Maybe you made it into adulthood before the window was cracked. But then the pebble came.

Was it a phone call? "We have your daughter at the station, you'd better come down here."

Was it a letter on the kitchen table? "I've left. Don't try to reach me. Don't try to call me. It's over. I just don't love you anymore."

Was it a diagnosis from the doctor? "I'm afraid our news is not very good."

Was it a telegram? "We regret to inform you that your son is missing in action."[1]

Why do we end up feeling disappointed by God? Is it really because of Him, or could it be because of our own expectations? We have our own unexpressed agenda. We believe, "If God is God, then ..." But does our agenda match the teaching of Scripture? Those who believe in the sovereignty and caring nature of God have a better basis upon which to approach life.

A book that has spoken to me every time I've read it is Lewis Smedes' *How Can It Be All Right when Everything Is All Wrong?* He has been through life's tough times. His insights and sensitivity to life's crises and God's presence and involvement in our lives can answer many of our questions. One of his personal experiences describes how our theology helps us move through life's changes.

The other night, trying to sleep, I amused myself by trying to recall the most happy moments of my life. I let my mind skip and dance where it was led. I thought of leaping down from a rafter in a barn, down into a deep loft of sweet, newly mown hay. That was a superbly happy moment. But somehow my mind was also seduced to a scene some years ago that, as I recall it, must have been the most painful of my life. Our firstborn child was torn from our hands by what felt to me like a capricious deity I did not want to call God. I felt ripped off by a cosmic con-artist. And for a little while, I thought I might not easily ever smile again.

But then, I do not know how, in some miraculous shift in my perspective, a strange and inexpressible sense came to me that my life, our lives, were still good, that life is good because it is *given*, and that its possibilities were still incalculable. Down into the gaps of feeling left over from the pain came a sense of givenness that nothing explains. It can only be felt as a gift of grace. An irrepressible impulse of blessing came from my heart to God for his sweet gift. And that was joy ... in spite of pain. Looking back, it seems to me now that I have never again known so sharp, so severe, so saving a sense of gratitude and so deep a joy, or so honest.[2]

Chuck Swindoll always shares so realistically and helpfully about life's difficulties. He tells us how a crisis can impact us:

Crisis crushes. And in crushing, it often refines and purifies. You may be discouraged today because the crushing has not yet led to a surrender. I've stood beside too many of the dying, ministered to too many of the broken and bruised to believe that crushing is an end in itself. Unfortunately, however, it usually takes the brutal blows of affliction to soften and penetrate hard hearts. Even though such blows often seem unfair.[3]

Alexander Solzhenitsyn's admission illustrates what Chuck Swindoll was saying:

It was only when I lay there on rotting prison straw that I sensed within myself the first stirring of good. Gradually, it was disclosed to me that the line separating good and evil passes, not through states, nor between classes, nor between political parties either, but right through all human hearts. So, bless you, prison, for having been in my life.[4]

Solzhenitsyn's words provide a perfect illustration of the psalmist's instruction to us in Scripture:

> Before I was afflicted I went astray,
> but now I obey your word....
> It was good for me to be afflicted
> so that I might learn your decrees.
>
> PSALMS 119:67,71, NIV

After crisis crushes sufficiently, God steps in to comfort and teach.

It's true that once crisis hits, your life will never be exactly the way it was! A crisis is like a bomb that sprays its lethal projectiles all around without regard for anyone standing in its way. The haunting words of an old children's game reflect the fallout of a crisis.

> Ring around the rosie
> Pocketful of posies
> Ashes, ashes
> All fall down.

But if we let Him, God uses the fallout from crisis to refine and hone our sense of His love toward us and His sovereignty in our lives.

The feelings you experience in a crisis come as waves. The earthquake intensity of any crisis recedes, and then the tidal waves of emotions begin their hammering process. And they keep rolling in, wave after wave.

These feelings have to have an outlet. If not, they won't stay buried. One day they will explode with a vengeance. One author describes it well:

I will never forget the time my dad left a can of aerosol spray in the back window of the family car while he was playing golf. The sun pounded on the window for a couple of hours and then the can detonated, shattering the windows and slicing a hole in the steel roof of the car. The force was unimaginable.

It's the same way with unexpressed feelings born in the midst of crisis. They fester and fester until they explode, adding damage to damage, doing nothing to reduce the problem.[5]

The father who described the loss of three of his family members in the first chapter reflects on the turmoil of his feelings.

Can anyone really expect to recover from such tragedy, considering the value of what was lost and the consequences of that loss? Recovery is a misleading and empty expectation. We recover from broken limbs, not amputations. Catastrophic loss by definition precludes recovery. It will transform us or destroy us, but it will never leave us the same. There is no going back to the past, which is gone forever, only going ahead to the future, which has yet to be discovered. Whatever that future is, it will, and must, include the pain of the past with it. Sorrow never entirely leaves the soul of those who have suffered a severe loss. If anything, it may keep going deeper.

But this depth of sorrow is the sign of a healthy soul, not a sick soul. It does not have to be morbid and fatalistic. It is not something to escape but something to embrace. Jesus said, "Blessed are those who mourn, for they will be comforted." Sorrow indicates that people who have suffered loss are living authentically in a world of misery, and it expresses the emotional anguish of people who feel pain for themselves or for others.[6]

Perhaps this chapter has been reflective of some of your life experiences. Perhaps you've walked through a problem that turned into a crisis and you now understand what factors led up to it and what intensified it. Or it could be that this chapter was a window into the future for you, since your crises have yet to hit.

It's true what Gerald Sittser said in the last quote that a crisis will either destroy us or transform us. Isn't it sad that the first lesson most of us learn about crisis is when we experience it? Why weren't we taught about the reality of crisis and its characteristics, and prepared to handle crisis, before it hits?

Survivors—those with *resilience*—are the people who understand the meaning of crisis, the typical ways of responding to a crisis, and the stages a person will experience as he or she walks through it. As you read the next chapter you will realize that what you've experienced in your crisis times is normal. This knowledge not only brings a sense of relief but provides help in becoming a person of resilience.

THREE

— ◆ —

"Am I Normal?"

Recognizing the Pattern of Crisis

You open your eyes but you can't see clearly. You blink. Everything is hazy, as though you were in a thick fog. There's a sense of unreality in everything around you. You feel as though you've been run over by a three-ton truck. You blink again, but your view of the world is still a bit fuzzy. Are you losing your mind? Were you in an accident? Did someone hit you? Probably none of the above.

Welcome to the world of experiencing crisis! When you and I enter into that state called "crisis time" we feel as though we've grabbed hold of a live electrical wire! As you read about the four phases inherent in a crisis, keep in mind that the time to transition through each phase will vary for each individual. Don't compare your experience with the approximate time suggested for getting through each phase. You could experience an intense crisis that prolongs a certain stage for months. And if you face another crisis before resolving the first one, the situation is compounded, further delaying each stage .

Why is it important to know about the phases of a crisis? By knowing what the four phases are, you will:

- realize that you're not going crazy, you're going through a normal passage;
- relieve some of the pain and pressure by recalling that, "Oh, yes, this phase will pass and I will go on to the next one";
- recognize there's light at the end of the tunnel—there is hope;
- gain control of your life and the outcome a bit sooner by knowing what to expect.

As writer Ann Stearns put it:

Recovery from loss is like having to get off the main highway every so many miles because the fire route is under reconstruction. The road signs reroute you through little towns you hadn't expected to visit and over bumpy roads you hadn't wanted to bounce around on. You are basically traveling in the appropriate direction. On the map, however, the course you are following has the look of shark's teeth instead of a straight line. Although you are gradually getting there, you sometimes doubt that you will ever meet up with the finished highway. There is a finished highway in your future. You won't know when or where, but it is there. You will discover a greater sense of resilience when you know in advance what you will experience and that you're normal in your response.[1]

The Impact Phase

The first stage of a crisis is called the impact phase. The intensity of a person's response to a crisis varies, but all of us feel the impact of a crisis. You know immediately that something drastic has happened to you. You're stunned. It's as if someone has hit you over the head with a two-by-four and you're seeing stars.

In chapter one you read an account of a father who had been in a car accident that killed three family members. He describes his feelings of horror and shock. He was in the impact stage when life appears to be falling apart with no hope for relief.

For some who see the crisis unfolding before them, there's a sense of panic and fear. This happens even to those who are observers of an impending crisis. The "Oh, no!" response is normal when you see a major tragedy about to occur and there's nothing you can do to stop it. I've experienced this more than once.

Years ago I was driving home in the late afternoon from teaching my classes at the graduate school at Biola University. I turned onto Stage Road, which ran parallel to the Amtrak train tracks, and then made another turn onto a cross street. Because a train was due in less than a minute, the arms at the train crossing had come down on the cross street.

As I sat waiting in line, several drivers became impatient and began to drive around the crossing arm and across the tracks. Out of the corner of my eye I saw the passenger train hurtling down the track as a VW Beetle began to sneak across. In that split second I knew what was going to happen. And with that knowledge I let out an anguished cry of "Oh, no!"

Then it happened. The train plowed into the small car and dragged the twisted metal hundreds of feet along the track. Turning my car out of the line of stopped traffic, I drove to a pay phone and called for help. As I drove home my mind and body were in shock. I think I prayed and talked out loud the entire way home.

When I got home I saw my wife Joyce and our daughter by the car. Sheryl had her driving permit and was getting into the driver's seat. I pulled up, got out of the car and said to them, "Sheryl is *not* driving anywhere today!" then went into the house. They were shocked at my outburst and followed me inside. They found me in the family room, pacing back and forth. I started to tell them what had happened, expressing my horror through tears. It took some time for the crash images to lose their sense of reality.

The next day I learned that the driver was a young Biola student and the daughter of one of the professors there. Fortunately she survived, although it took her months to recover.

Another time I had just walked into my bedroom and heard a helicopter flying overhead. The sound wasn't the normal pitch of the engine, so I rushed outside. I looked up and saw the helicopter twisting and turning as it flew on, apparently out of control. It continued to veer one way and then another as the pilot fought to maintain control. About a mile away the helicopter plunged straight down. During this time, I was saying, "Oh, no! It can't be!" Part of my worry came from its proximity to a friend's home.

Later I learned that tragedy was averted when the craft hit wires that broke its fall. The three occupants escaped with minor injuries. But I still experienced that state of pain and panic.

In recalling a crisis experience in his own life, Gordon MacDonald wrote,

I will never forget those first days. It was almost impossible to ward off the feeling that life was over, that all the brightness and joy that we had known for more than forty-five years had come to a screeching halt.

Our worlds were broken. A dream had turned into a nightmare of loss, humiliation, anger, and a sense of a very dark future. There was the terrible realization that many who had trusted me were now disillusioned. There was the knowledge that some people were talking, with or without a knowledge of the facts.

At one point I felt as though the ground was opening beneath me! Like if I were to look down the world was going to swallow me up.[2]

MacDonald isn't alone in his dramatic description of the crisis phase. Others have expressed it this way:

"I felt like I was in a free fall. But I didn't have a parachute!"

"It was a strange sensation. I sort of felt as though the world was somehow less real, like I was disconnected, except of course when it came crashing in on me. It was that kind of alternating experience: Sometimes I was 'out of it'; sometimes I was in the middle of it; but I could never get away from it."

"There was this growing sense of powerlessness."[3]

The Length of the Impact

The impact phase is usually brief, lasting from a few hours to a few days, depending upon the event and the person involved. Some impact phases linger on and on, such as in the case of a divorce proceeding. If you can identify with the words of these examples above, you may be in this phase now.

The more severe the crisis or loss, the greater the impact and the greater the amount of incapacitation and numbness. Tears may be an immediate part of this phase or they may be expressed later on.

During this phase, one of the questions you must answer is, "Should I stay and face the problem or withdraw and run from it?" This is called the fight-or-flight pattern.

A few years back, an advertisement espoused the words, "I'd rather fight than switch." Not everyone feels that way in a crisis. If your tendency in the past has been to face problems, you will probably face your crisis head-on. But if your tendency has been to avoid or withdraw from problems, you will probably run from your next crisis. If the crisis is especially severe, you may feel like running anyway, because you're not as able to cope during the impact phase.

Most of the time, running from a crisis is not the solution. It merely prolongs the situation. And since there are three more phases of a crisis yet to come before balance is restored, why linger in the impact phase? Why prolong the pain? Facing a crisis and fighting to regain control is usually the healthier response.

Don't expect to do any clear thinking during the impact phase. You'll feel numb and disoriented. You may even feel as though you can't think or feel at all. Someone described it this way: "I feel as though my entire system shut down."

Your ability to process information is limited. If a friend or family member attempts to share any factual information with you, it sails right over your head. You may ask, "What did you say?" even though the person has repeated it for the third time. Don't despair when this happens. It's a normal response that everyone experiences.

It's best if you don't have to make any important decisions at this time, but if you do, ask a competent friend to help you.

At the Center of the Impact

At the heart of most crises is a loss of some kind. Losses threaten our security, our sense of stability, our well-being. Self-image may be affected, and you feel out of control. The more sudden the loss, the more out of control you will feel. Although a gradual loss is still painful, you can prepare for it to some degree. But a sudden, unexpected death may disrupt your ability to activate the emotional resources you need in order to cope with the loss.

One of the most difficult types of losses to deal with is the *threat* of loss. For some, it is like a crisis waiting to happen. The loss has not yet occurred, but there's a real possibility that it will happen.

Any kind of loss has a way of changing our lives in a dramatic way and affects the way we think about the future. These changes can be positive and eventually enrich our lives. But during the first few months of a crisis, it doesn't feel that way at all. If someone were to tell you at the time of a loss that you can learn and grow through it, you might react with disgust, anger or disbelief! You aren't ready to handle thoughts like that. You can only hear such comments when life is more stable.

During the impact phase, a person's thought life focuses on the loss in an effort to find what he or she has lost. It's normal to search for something that meant a great deal to you. You're trying to hold on to your emotional attachments for a bit longer. You're trying to recapture the lost dream, the loved one or even your health. The more your loss meant to you, the more you will search!

This searching behavior often takes the form of reminiscing. How much you reminisce is in proportion to the value of what you lost. It is common (and healthy) for a person who loses a loved one in death to pore over photographs and other items that remind him or her of the person who died.

Surviving the Impact

There are several things you can do to work through the impact stage of loss. In fact, these action steps will help you deal with your grief in a healthy way. What do you need to do most during the impact phase of a crisis?

1. You need to accept what has happened, accept your feelings and reminisce. Recently I was counseling a young woman who had lost her father six months before. She flew back east for the funeral, but had not gone back since. This meant that she had not had the opportunity to spend time in the home where her father lived or to reminisce with friends or other relatives. Because of this, her grief was blocked. I suggested that she write her mother and ask her to send the photograph album that contained pictures of her and her father. When it arrived, I encouraged her to sit down with a friend and look through the book and talk about the various experiences each picture portrayed. She needed to reminisce.

It's normal and healthy to express as many feelings as you can. It may be difficult at first to experience your feelings because of the numbness, but when the numbness wears off, your feelings can be intense. This intensity may increase and carry into the next phase. You may even find yourself emotionally exhausted.

2. You need a safe environment in which to grieve. Avoid those people who try to make you stifle your feelings. Feelings should not be buried or denied at this point, because rejected feelings delay the resolution of the problem. When feelings are buried, they do not go away, they are simply frozen.

Do you know what happens to water when it freezes? The ice actually expands. Water frozen in pipes has the power to burst those steel pipes wide open. When we lock up a summer mountain cabin for the winter, it's important to drain all of the water from the pipes if we want them to function properly the next spring. The analogy holds when we speak of frozen emotions. They can expand and take on a power out of proportion to their original nature, so it's important during grief and crisis to keep the channels open so that feelings can flow when they need to.

Avoid those people who are full of advice and say, "I told you so" or "Spiritual Christians get over their hurt sooner than others." Find people who are empathetic and know how to minister to you during a crisis. The people who can help you most have these qualities:

They don't shock easily but accept your human feelings.

They are not embarrassed by your tears.

They do not give unwanted advice.

They are warm and affectionate with you, according to your needs.

They help you recall your strengths when you've forgotten you have strengths.

They trust you to be able to come through this difficult time.

They treat you like an adult who can make your own decisions.

They may become angry with you, but they don't attack your character.

They respect your courage and sense of determination.

They understand that grief is normal and they understand the stages of grief.

They, too, may have been through times of difficulty and can share those times with you.

They do not spiritualize everything.

They are sensitive to where you are spiritually and do not try to force-feed you theology and Scripture.[4]

Cultivate friendships with these people *before* a crisis hits. But remember, we draw this kind of people to us as we demonstrate *we* are that kind of people, too.

Some people talk to release their feelings because that's what they know best. Others may empty themselves of their emotions in physical ways. We shouldn't compare ourselves with others and say one way of release is the only way or the best way. Some people talk about their hurt and grief; some act it out. You may have a friend who spends a great deal of time working in the yard or doing some other kind of activity but doesn't talk about the loss of her spouse. You may be concerned that she's not dealing with her loss, but she may be doing just that in her own way.

For some, rigorous physical activity can bring about the healing. I heard of a man who lost his father in a tragic fire. He lived near his father on an adjacent farm. One night the home in which he was born and raised burned to the ground with his father inside. His response to this tragedy startled other family members. He remained silent while they all wept and talked about the loss. Then he borrowed a bulldozer and proceeded to bulldoze the ashes and charred remains of the house.

The rain had stopped the fire, and this was his one expression of burying his father. He worked for hours, not even stopping for meals or rest. When darkness came, he continued to work, ignoring the requests of family members to stop for the night. Instead he continued to bulldoze the remains back and forth, again and again.

This man and his father were farmers, and for most of their lives they had worked together in the fields. They didn't verbalize much together nor share their feelings. But theirs was a close nonverbal relationship.

You and I may grieve with tears. He grieved with his borrowed bulldozer. This was his personal expression of words and tears. He cried by working the land over and over again until nothing was visible. He gave his father and the home a proper burial in his own way. The land, which in a sense was his father's cemetery, was now ready to be farmed, and it would be—by the son.

If you were to ask this man why he had done this, he couldn't give you an answer. He didn't know why he had acted out his grief in this way, but he had done something with his grief, and it was probably the best thing he could have done.

The more immobilized you are by your grief, the more dependent and helpless you feel. Doing something—anything—whether it makes sense to anyone else or not is a healthy step. It assists you as a beginning step to feeling you have some control again.

3. Be aware that guilt may become your unwelcome companion. Sometimes guilt causes us to respond in a variety of ways we wouldn't normally respond, from rationalizing and blaming to self-punishment or attempts at atonement. Guilt may try to consume you.

Let me tell you about Sarah. She was rich. Very, very rich. Not only was her income a thousand dollars a day, but she had inherited twenty million. That's not bad ... especially in the late 1800s. By today's standards, she could have been a billionaire. She was well known in high society. Just mention her name and everyone knew her. She was invited to every social event or party. And she had power. Her name opened doors and opportunities. She was sought after by boards, lenders, politicians. They wanted her support and money.

Sarah had it all ... including misery. Her only child had died at five weeks, and then her husband had died. Two losses and two potential crises. She was alone. She had her name, her memories and her money. There was something else she had as well—quiet. To get away she moved from Connecticut to San Jose, California.

She purchased an eight-room farmhouse as well as the adjoining 160 acres. But then a strange thing happened. She hired sixteen carpenters to work on her house, twenty-four hours a day, every day, for the next thirty-eight years. The layout of the house, to put it in today's vernacular, was weird. Each window had thirteen panes, each wall thirteen panels, each closet thirteen hooks and each chandelier thirteen globes.

The floor plan was bizarre. Corridors were put in at random. Some led nowhere. A set of stairs led to a ceiling that had no door, and one door opened to a blank wall. There were tunnels, trap-doors and secret passageways. The work on this mysterious mansion finally came to a halt when Sarah died. But after thirty-eight years can you imagine what this house was like? It covered six acres and had the following features: six kitchens, thirteen bathrooms, forty stairways, forty-seven fireplaces, fifty-two skylights, 467 doors, ten thousand windows, 160 rooms and one bell tower.

What would drive a wealthy woman to become so eccentric, so driven, so compulsive? After all, she didn't need what she built. She lived alone. Or did she? A legend evolved that said Sarah Winchester had "visitors" every night. The story goes that a servant would go to the bell tower at night via a secret passage and ring the bell. Sarah would then go into the "blue room," which was reserved for her and her guests, and stay there until 2:00 A.M. Then the bell would once again ring and the visitors would depart, and Sarah Winchester would go to her room.

The visitors? They were United States soldiers killed on the United States frontier. They were slain Indians torn apart by the bullets that struck them. Both soldiers and Indians were killed by that new invention, the repeating Winchester rifle. It brought millions of dollars to the Winchester family but death to thousands of others. It also brought haunting experiences to Sarah Winchester prompted by a guilt that went unresolved. To atone for what had occurred she tried to provide a home for the dead.[5]

Expressions of Self-Blame

Isn't it interesting how we tend to hook into guilt and end up pointing the finger back at ourselves? Self-blame is usually unrealistic and harsher than the blame we place on others. Our imagination takes the event and magnifies our sense of responsibility. We tell ourselves things like, "If only ..." or "I should have ..." Listen to some of the statements common to self-blame:

"If only I hadn't allowed him to buy that motorcycle. If only I'd insisted he wear his helmet, he wouldn't be paralyzed now. I should have been home that night. If I'd been there, the accident wouldn't have happened."

"I kick myself all over for not telling Mom I loved her. She's not here now and I can't let her know. That opportunity is gone forever."

"If I hadn't spent so much time at work, she wouldn't have left me. I was just trying to provide, but I guess I blew it. I kick myself again and again."

"I should have noticed his depression. I just didn't believe what he was saying, and now he's dead. By his own hand."

"Where did we go wrong with that child? I guess we were too young and too ignorant. We blew it and she's in trouble because of us."

Let's summarize what happens to you during the impact phase, which may take a few hours or even a few days. During the impact phase you will want to face the situation and fight, or you'll want to flee; you will think in a somewhat numb and disoriented fashion; you will search for whatever it is you have lost, often by reminiscing; you will need people to accept your feelings.

The Withdrawal-Confusion Phase

After the impact phase you're going to move into the withdrawal-confusion phase. This will last for days or even weeks, and you will feel emotionally drained. You are worn out. Remember, the various phases overlap one another and you may move between different phases. That too is normal.

During the confusion-withdrawal phase the tendency to deny your feelings is probably stronger than at any other time. One reason is because your feelings now can become the ugliest and most potent. As one emotion triggers another, you may feel intense anger at whatever has occurred, which in some cases brings on guilt for having such feelings. Then you feel shame. The pain from these varied responses increases your desire to repress them. If some of your feelings shock others, you may want to repress them even more.

Expect your feelings to run wild. This is a normal response. In fact, you will probably feel a sense of

- bewilderment: "I never felt this way before."
- danger: "I feel so scared. Something terrible is going to happen."
- confusion: "I can't think clearly. My mind doesn't seem to work."
- impasse: "I'm stuck. Nothing I do seems to help."
- desperation: "I've got to do something, but I don't know what to do."
- apathy: "Nothing can help me. What's the use of trying?"
- helplessness: "I can't cope by myself. Please help me."
- urgency: "I need help *now*."
- discomfort: "I feel so miserable and unhappy."

During the withdrawal-confusion phase your thinking patterns will reflect a certain amount of uncertainty and ambiguity. You just aren't sure what to think or do.

You will alternate between bargaining and detachment. Bargaining involves wishful thinking: "If only this hadn't happened"; "If only I could recapture what I had"; "Perhaps there's some way to bring back what I had."

This type of thinking then moves to the detachment level. You need to detach yourself from whatever it was you lost, whether it is a job, a friend or a spouse. A widower cannot stay married to a deceased wife. An expelled student can no longer be a student in the school from which he was expelled. A worker cannot fulfill a job he or she has lost. You distance yourself by saying, "It wasn't that important"; "I can do better now that he or she isn't in my life anymore"; "I wanted a new job anyway." You do this to ease the pain of your loss.

You may find yourself vacillating between performing some tasks that need to be done and then reflecting and reminiscing upon how things used to be. You may feel anger at having to give up what you lost, whether it is a person, an object or an identity. We try to protect ourselves from the emptiness that loss brings. In our attempt to restore what is gone, we tend to distort and glorify the past. We do this to help us face the future. As we reach out to new tasks and even to new people, we do it in an attempt to fill the void in our lives.

During this time you need the assistance of caring friends and relatives to help you organize your life. You will probably need assistance in planning your day, arranging appointments, keeping the house or job in order and so on. Don't be hard on yourself for this apparent defect in your life. It's a normal transition through your grief. The period of grief over the loss of a spouse is not the time to be looking for another partner. It's a time to adjust to the loss.

Secondary Wounding

There is one additional source of pain you'll need to contend with—other people who make statements that hurt rather than console, hinder rather than comfort, and prolong your pain rather than relieve it. These people are secondary wounders. They will give you unwanted and bad advice as well as improperly applied Scripture. You won't be the first to experience this. Remember Job?

[Job] had four well-meaning but insufferable friends who came over to cheer him up and try to explain [his suffering]. They said that anybody with enough sense to come in out of the rain knew that God was just. They said that anybody old enough to spell his own name knew that since God was just, he made bad things happen to bad people and good things happen to good people. They said that such being the case, you didn't need a Harvard diploma to figure out that since bad things had happened to Job, then *ipso facto* he must have done something bad himself. But Job hadn't, and he said so, and that's not all he said either. "Worthless physicians are you all," he said. "Oh that you would keep silent, and it would be your wisdom" (Job 13:4-5). They were a bunch of theological quacks, in other words, and the smartest thing they could do was shut up. But they were too busy explaining things to listen.[6]

Moralizing is not the same as spiritual wisdom. Those who don't know what to say violate what the Book of Proverbs instructs us to do and offer clichés and untruths instead. Look at the truth of Proverbs:

Don't talk so much. You keep putting your foot in your mouth. Be sensible and turn off the flow!   Proverbs 10:19, TLB

Some people like to make cutting remarks, but the words of the wise soothe and heal.   Proverbs 12:18, TLB

The tongue of the wise utters knowledge rightly, but the mouth of the [self-confident] fool pours out folly.   Proverbs 15:2. AMP

Death and life are in the power of the tongue, and they who indulge it shall eat the fruit of it [for death or life].   PROVERBS 18:21, AMP

A wise man scales the city of the mighty, and brings down the stronghold in which they trust.   PROVERBS 21:22, NASB

Just expect to hear statements you'd rather not hear. It's difficult to respond to these people the way we would like to because of our traumatized state. Perhaps they would learn not to make such harmful statements if someone spoke up and said, "That's not true and it's not helpful. If you want to be helpful I would appreciate it if you would … " Sometimes we excuse what these people say as well-meaning, which is questionable. Sometimes they're just reflecting their own anxiety, fear or lack of having dealt with issues in their own lives. Remember, this is not advice coming from experts.

Consider some typical clichés we hear from others when we go through a crisis.

"Be Strong" Clichés

- Big boys don't cry.
- The children are flexible … they will bounce back.
- You must be strong for the children.
- Support groups are for wimps.
- You've just got to get hold of yourself!
- Others have held up well. You can, too.
- Cheer up.
- No sense crying over spilt milk.
- This is nature's way.

"Hurry Up" Clichés

- You're not your old self.
- Out of sight, out of mind.
- Time will heal.
- You're young, and you'll be able to make a new life for yourself.
- I just don't understand your behavior.

- Life goes on.
- No sense dwelling on the past.

"Guilt" Clichés

- If you look around, you can always find someone who is worse off than you.
- This is the work of the devil (meaning that if you had a closer relationship with God the devil couldn't have had his way).
- If I were you I'd do it this way.
- Count your blessings.
- Only the good die young.
- If you had been a better Christian, this wouldn't have happened to you.
- Think of all your precious memories.
- It's a blessing.

"God" Clichés

- God needs him more than you do.
- He's happy now because he's with God.
- God did this to show how powerful He can be in your life.
- It was God's will.
- God never gives us more than we can handle.
- God helps those who help themselves.

"Discounting" Clichés

- I know just how you feel.
- Silence is golden.
- If there's anything I can do, just call me.
- You can have more children.
- It's better to have loved and lost than never to have loved at all.
- Be glad you don't have problems like mine.
- What you don't know won't hurt you.[7]

Those who share with you in this manner need to be avoided or educated! During this phase, when the numbness has worn off, you begin to feel the pain of hearing comments such as these.

To summarize, in the withdrawal-confusion phase (which will last for days, sometimes for weeks), your response will be emotional. You may feel anger, fear, guilt, even rage. Your thinking processes feel muddled. You will vacillate from bargaining to working on detaching yourself from the lost person or situation.

During this time of puzzled searching for a way out of the difficulty, you need some task-oriented support and help from others. You need others to help you make some plans and accomplish small tasks so that you can feel functional. Don't hesitate to let others know that you want to do something or that you need to feel useful.

The Adjustment Phase

The third phase, called the adjustment phase, will take weeks to work through. But the emotional responses you experience during this time are focused toward hope. Yes, you may feel some depression that comes and goes, but you've started to form positive attitudes again. You may begin to talk about the future with hope and look forward to enjoying a new job, moving to a new location, rebuilding a fire-destroyed home, considering remarriage. You've just about completed your detachment from what you've lost. You are looking around for something new to which you can develop an attachment.

Your future dreams or action steps start to take on special significance to you. You've been in and through the depths of the valley and you're now climbing up the side of the mountain. Be prepared for the opinions and advice of others and sift through what you hear.

Others may not see the value of what you are doing now. They could question your decisions and actions if what you're doing doesn't jive with what they think you need to do. Some people may feel that you're making a drastic mistake as you take a new step.

Don't make any important decisions during your down times; wait until you feel hope. And don't despair because your feelings fluctuate. Your insight is returning and your objectivity can help you process information and new suggestions.

Scripture can assist you in making decisions during this phase. You're more receptive now and capable of dealing with spiritual insights. Prior to this point, Scripture and prayer resources were there to support and sustain you. Now is the time to seek answers and direction through the teaching and reading of the Word.

The Reconstruction-Reconciliation Phase

The final phase (which can last the longest) is the reconstruction-reconciliation phase. A key element here is your spontaneous expressions of hope. Your sense of confidence has returned and you can make plans again. You're able to consciously decide not to engage in self-pity anymore.

Initiative, progress and *reattachment* are key words during this period of time. You've assimilated into your life new places, new activities, new people, new jobs and new spiritual insights. If your feelings of anger and blame created difficulty during this crisis, now is the time to reconcile with those people you may have offended.

One sign of crisis resolution is the newness of life you feel and the new discoveries you experience. A crisis is an opportunity for you to gain new strengths, new perspectives on life, new appreciation, new values and a new way to approach the way you live. You will look at life differently. Hopefully, you will not take it for granted. I know this firsthand.

Several years ago I experienced some strange physical symptoms. These included vertigo, pressure in the back of the head and headaches. These symptoms persisted for about seven weeks, during which time the doctors had some theories but nothing concrete. My own concerns and worries about what this might be added to some of the feelings I experienced.

Finally, after going through further examinations, including a CAT scan, the symptoms disappeared. As we pieced together what had occurred, we felt the physical symptoms were brought on by too many strenuous seminars with no recuperation time in between, coupled with a cold and some altitude changes.

Physical exhaustion is one of the greatest culprits of mysterious ailments. But this experience, especially at the age of forty-seven, caused me to think, reevaluate and consider some changes in my life. I learned to pace my work in a more balanced manner. I learned to play more and evaluate what was important and what wasn't. I began to say no. I didn't necessarily like what I went through, but I grew because of it and felt it was a necessary experience.

Crisis and trials can become the means to exciting growth. I've always been impressed with William Pruitt and his response to a physical problem he conquered. In many ways his crisis was with him for the rest of his life. In his book *Run from the Pale Pony*, Pruitt uses an analogy to describe what happened in his life. In the foreword of the book he writes:

About thirty years ago, one of my joys as a boy was to ride a white horse named Prince. That proud, spirited stallion carried me where I wanted to go, wherever I bid him to and at the pace which I chose. I don't have to explain to horsemen the feeling of strength, even authority, which comes from controlling such a powerful animal. Nor need I expand upon the excitement I felt when I galloped him at full speed, or about the quiet pride that came when I twisted him through the corkscrew turns of a rodeo exercise. After all, he was mine and I trained him. Those experiences are a part of my heritage.

My cherished white horse was gone and seldom remembered about fifteen years later. It was then that I encountered a completely different kind of horse. When I first became aware of the specter, its shape was too dim to discern. I know only that I had never seen anything like it before. Too, I know that I had not sought any such creature, yet something different was with me wherever I went and that shadow would not go away. No matter what I did, though, the specter followed my every move. Furthermore, the harder I tried to lose it, the clearer the creature's form became to me.

My uneasiness changed to anxiety when I realized that this unwanted shadow had a will of its own. The chill of fear came when I understood that it had no intention of leaving me alone. Without further warning, it began to communicate with me openly one day, and in a harsh voice which was almost rigid with animosity, it spat out, "You can no longer go where you want to go when you choose at the speed you pick. That's true because I will give you weakness instead of strength. Excitement and pride? Never again will you have them like before. I plan only confinement and disability for you. And I will be your constant companion. My name is Chronic Illness."

At the time I heard it speak, I shrank back from actually seeing it face to face. It spoke harshly of miseries which were inverse to joys with my white horse named Health and the bitter irony was reflected in the form of a malicious creature. Chronic Illness took the shape of a stunted, misshapen pony. Its shaggy coat was pale in color, streaked with ages-old accumulation of dark despair. But, unquestionably, the most frightening feature of the animal was its overwhelming glare, its glare-eyed stare which held me helpless. The pony's wild eyes stared restlessly from side to side, yet strangely were unbinding. This book is written first of all for those people who have met the pale pony face to face.[8]

The "pale pony" might come in many possible forms—serious physical or mental illness, accident, war or other injuries. Whatever shape the pony takes, the results can be quite similar. William Pruitt's pale pony was multiple sclerosis. He sensed that the disease was increasingly affecting his life, but his story is the story of hope. He realized that he had a number of years before he would be completely disabled, and realizing that he wouldn't be able to carry on the type of work he was in, he went back to college in a wheelchair. He earned a Ph.D. in economics and began to teach on a college level.

Pruitt's book is not about giving up; rather it is about fighting back and winning. It is a very honest book, telling of the pain and the hurt and the turmoil. But its emphasis is on faith and hope.

You may not be able to do what you used to do; your life might not return to the way it was. But you can look for alternatives. You can discover alternate ways of responding. You can learn to say, "I will be able to *discover* plan 'B.' There *is* a different way to live my life!"

When you find yourself (or someone else) experiencing a crisis, look at the "Normal Crisis Pattern" chart on page 52. In fact, make a photocopy and keep it handy (perhaps in your Bible) for personal use or to help others when they are in need. This chart will help remind you that your feelings are normal and there is hope and light at the end of the tunnel.

Remember, too, that a crisis is an opportunity! It is a time for change and growth. There is one factor—attitude—that causes a major crisis to become a growth-producing experience instead of a restrictive, crippling, eternal tragedy. Our world is unstable; it rocks our boat. We are unstable; we rock our boat. But if our attitude has been built upon the teachings of the Word of God, that is our hope in the midst of an upset world! Isaiah 33:6 says, "And He shall be the stability of your times."

Our stability comes from allowing Jesus Christ to be our rock at all times.

The Normal Crisis Pattern

Emotional Level

	Phase I Impact	Phase II Withdrawal Confusion	Phase III Adjustment	Phase IV Reconstruction/Reconciliation
	Time–Few hours to a few days	Days to weeks	Weeks to months	Months
Response	Should I stay and face it or withdraw?	Intense emotions. You feel drained. Anger, sadness, fear, anxiety, depression, rage, guilt.	Your positive thoughts begin returning along with all the emotions.	Hope has returned. Self confidence.
Thoughts	Numb, disoriented. Insight ability limited. Feelings overwhelm.	Thinking ability limited. Uncertainty and ambiguity.	You're now able to problem solve.	Thinking is clearer.
Direction you take to regain control	You search for what you lost.	Bargaining-wishful thinking. Detachment.	You begin looking for something new to invest in.	Progress is evident and new attachments are made to something significant.
Searching behavior	Often Reminiscing.	Puzzled, unclear.	You can now stay focused and begin to learn from your experience.	You may want to stop and evaluate where you've been and where you're going.

FOUR

— ◆ —

"Why Do I Feel This Way?"

Reading the Message in Painful Emotions

They hit with the intensity of a tornado and the suddenness of an earthquake. They won't go away when you want them to, and there's no way to evict them. They're like a runaway train whose brakes have burned out. You feel totally out of control. Even though you may question the necessity of their presence, they do have a purpose. What do we call these "unfriendly" companions? *Emotions. Feelings.*

You may experience many kinds of emotions during a crisis, and perhaps some feelings you've never felt before. It's not just the presence of emotions that bothers you, it's their intensity.

When you understand that feeling an emotion is an unavoidable human condition, and you know what to expect from emotions, you will handle them better. Many people feel they alone experience such intense feelings. This misbelief keeps them from accepting their feelings, learning from them and moving on to recovery. Which emotions are your most frequent companions?

Anger

Anger is a sign of protest. It's a natural and predictable emotion after a crisis or loss. It's a reaction against something that shouldn't have happened. It's a way of fighting back when you feel helpless. Your perception of the way things are or the way they should be has been altered. Your belief system has been damaged. Anger is a normal reaction when you are deprived of something you value.

Expressions of anger against the injustices of life have always been with us. We find anger expressed in the psalms and the books of the prophets. Job expressed anger at God, as did Jonah and Elijah.

Hundreds of years ago the American Indians shot arrows into the air to drive away evil spirits. We still do this, but we do it in a different way. We shake our fists, we verbalize, we write letters and, in some cases, we file lawsuits.

Sometimes we run into problems with anger. Society doesn't always know how to respond to our anger, and neither do many people in the church. That's because they often have an incorrect perspective of Scripture on this subject and they attempt to project that perspective on others.

Let's take a look at some of the typical ways we direct our anger to avoid dealing with the pain.

Anger at God

Too often there is no appropriate object on which to vent our anger, so we begin looking for anything! Whom do we get angry at most often? God. We blame Him—He shouldn't have done this or He shouldn't have allowed that. He's supposed to do things right, which means according to the way we want it!

When you blame God, it can be unnerving and unsettling to other people, so they either respond with Christian clichés or try to convince you that your anger at God is irrational. They fail to realize that nothing they say will help, because you are living on emotions at this point. Even though you may be raising questions, you're not really looking for answers.

People who are resilient in a crisis vent their anger rather than stuff it. They realize that to deny anger buries it alive and someday there will be a resurrection. Buried anger can lead to addiction, alcohol abuse and depression. But when anger is expressed to God it can be analyzed, dealt with and can lead to a rediscovery of the character and purposes of God.

Anger at the Unfairness of Life

You may be angry at the unfairness of the world—the unfairness of life itself. In 1995 in Los Angeles, a trash truck pulled alongside a school bus loaded with children. A part on the lift apparatus malfunctioned and a large steel beam shot through the window of the bus, killing two young students instantly. Why them? Why so young? Why not the irresponsible ones? We raise these questions in vain. Because they are unanswerable, anger, disillusionment and even irrationality become part of our emotional state.

After the crash of TWA Flight 800 into the waters off Long Island, New York, there was an outburst of anger from many fronts. That day a small town in Pennsylvania lost several high school students and chaperons on their way to France for two weeks of study. Even one death in a small community is felt by almost everyone, but when several are killed, the whole community plunges into crisis. The unfairness of losing so many from a small area generates an outburst against the unfairness of the world.

Anger at Others

Our anger may also be directed toward other people. Family members of those killed on TWA Flight 800 voiced their anger over the slowness with which victims were recovered and the announcement of details from the media rather than being notified directly. They were angry at TWA, the media, the recovery workers and the politicians.

We get angry at those who haven't had to experience what we've gone through. Because they haven't experienced, or we think they haven't experienced, the devastation that we have, part of us wants them to experience the same thing.

Because we believe the tragedy or crisis shouldn't have happened, we look for something or someone to blame—a doctor, a hospital, an organization, a CEO, accountant, bus driver or anyone we perceive as having somehow participated in the crisis. Sometimes our anger is vented toward anyone who is around, especially family members.

People get angry at the physician who helped a loved one. Fire and flood victims get angry at the police and firefighters who failed to save their homes. Widows often feel anger toward close family members after the first few weeks of bereavement. They feel overprotected, overcontrolled, or they feel a lack of support as well as disappointment in the expected assistance from others.

You may get angry at those who fail to reach out and support you during your time of trouble. When we hurt, we want to be acknowledged. We don't want people to pretend that everything is okay. Because it isn't. And in some cases it never will be the same. Of course, part of the reason we end up feeling isolated is because no one has bothered to help others know how to minister to us during a time of need. Fortunately, this is starting to change.

Anger at Self

You may direct your anger inward. Women are more likely to do this, while men generally turn anger outward. Anger turned inward is quite common after physical loss, as well as when one is the victim of a crime. Intense self-directed anger can be immobilizing.

Sometimes, if your crisis was the death of a loved one, you may feel anger at the one who died. Survivors sometimes feel deserted or victimized. The loss of a spouse or a parent may leave you with the responsibility of what they left undone. Often anger comes because we feel out of control, powerless and victimized.

How do you deal with anger in a positive way? You admit it, you accept it, you release it in a healthy way. You use anger's energy to do something constructive. Mothers Against Drunk Drivers (MADD) was founded because of the constructive use of anger directed toward a major problem in our society—those who drink and drive. The MADD organization has made society aware of the problem of drunk drivers on our roads and highways and has helped to establish and reinforce laws to prosecute those who victimize others through their negligence. MADD uses its anger as energy to correct a major societal problem. There are other examples.

A family who lost their son in a drowning accident at a lake organized a group of parents to convince resort owners and fish and game officials to post warning signs about water conditions to reduce the possibility of other similar events occurring.

A young mother whose two-year-old died in the cancer ward of a hospital developed a program of cooperation among fifteen churches in the city to set up support groups for parents of early childhood death. In addition, each church solicited huge toy donations from merchants and families for the hospital pediatric ward.

Actress Theresa Saldano almost lost her life in a premeditated violent attack. She was stabbed again and again, requiring over a thousand stitches in her body. The attack left her with feelings of terror, intense pain and rage. In her book *Beyond Survival* she said it was her rage that gave her the energy to fight pain, death and the sick desires of her assailant. It was also her rage at the treatment victims receive in our society that gave her the vision to form a victim advocacy group called "Victims for Victims."

I don't know if anger over the accident that paralyzed him is what prompted Christopher Reeve to accomplish what he has. But he's worked hard to gain financial support, increase public and government awareness and lobby for new legislation to help spinal cord-damaged victims. He has written each United States senator personally, and has helped to raise millions of dollars for research on this problem.[1]

Perhaps you could write a letter (don't mail it!) to whomever you're angry at and then sit in a room and read it aloud. Many people have found release by journaling each day to release pent-up feelings of anger. The point is, those who are resilient come to grips with their anger in constructive ways.

A friend of mine, Jessica Shaver, wrote the following poem that depicts what so many people have discovered.

I Told God I Was Angry

I told God I was angry.
I thought He'd be surprised.
I thought I'd kept hostility
quite cleverly disguised.

I told the Lord I hate Him.
I told Him that I hurt.
I told Him that He isn't fair,
He's treated me like dirt.

I told God I was angry
but *I'm* the one surprised.
"What I've known all along,"
He said,
"you've finally realized.

"At last you have admitted
what's really in your heart.
Dishonesty, not anger,
was keeping us apart.

"Even when you hate Me
I don't stop loving you.
Before you can receive
that love
you must confess what's true.

"In telling me the anger
you genuinely feel,
It loses power over you,
permitting you to heal."

I told God I was sorry
and He's forgiven me.
The truth that I was angry
has finally set me free.

Guilt

Another companion of crisis is guilt. This is a normal response and can often be traced to our tendency to place blame, only now we end up pointing the finger back at ourselves.

Guilt is present in any crisis when we feel that we've fallen short in some way or have violated something we believe in. Often the standards we set for ourselves are based upon unrealistic and inappropriate expectations.

Crisis brought on by the loss of another person, whether it's through a broken relationship, divorce or death, often moves us into a selective memory mode. That is, we tend to remember everything that was negative in our relationship while failing to recall the positive. Initially in this type of loss we tend to dwell on the negative things we contributed to the relationship and overstate the good things the other person contributed.

Guilt grows when we repeat the "if onlys," "could haves," "should haves," and "shouldn't haves." I've heard statements like "I should have known CPR," "I shouldn't have let him ride that motorcycle" or "If only I'd had the radio on I would have heard the tornado warning."

This type of reaction is especially true when the loss involves a child. For example, after the crisis of a miscarriage or stillbirth, parents question themselves and each other. They wonder if it happened because of something they did or didn't do (more about this in chapter six).

When an adolescent chooses a different lifestyle or value system, a parent asks, "Where did I go wrong?" "Why didn't I spend more time with him?" "Why didn't I take more interest in his schoolwork?" "If only I had home-schooled him instead."

We may even feel guilty over some of the feelings we experience during the upset of a crisis. I've talked to many people who have said their guilt came because they doubted God, questioned God, didn't have enough faith, didn't believe enough, weren't spiritual enough. When guilt enters our life, whether it's realistic or exaggerated, we tend to develop an unhealthy preoccupation with how bad we are. We look at ourselves in a distorted way. We focus on our sinful state and fail to remember God's offer of forgiveness.

More and more today we hear about survivor guilt. Accidents, tornadoes, earthquakes and terrorist attacks create a special kind of remorse in those who were directly or only somewhat involved in the tragic event but survived. There were many survivors of the Oklahoma bombing with only minor injuries or no injuries at all. Many of them experienced survival guilt. Even some of the family members of those who were lost in TWA Flight 800 ended up asking, "Why them? It should have been me. They were too young. I'm older." This type of questioning often happens when the tragedy affects a well-known person or a child. The belief that it would have been more sensible for the tragedy to have happened to you rather than the other person is a clear indication of survivor guilt. At the heart of some of these feelings could be the belief that you were allowed to avoid the tragedy at the cost of the other person. That feeling is rarely anchored in fact.

A Resilient Response to Guilt

There are two kinds of guilt. Some call them good guilt and bad guilt; others call them legitimate guilt and illegitimate guilt. Guilt that is out of proportion to an event is the "bad" or "illegitimate" kind of guilt. Feeling this kind of guilt can be normal in a crisis that involves the loss of a significant person, and usually it comes from the unrealistic beliefs we hold, the "I should haves" that no one could ever attain.

The resilient individual talks over his or her feelings with a person holding an objective outlook on the situation. If the only one you're talking to about your guilt is yourself, remember, you are biased. A nonjudgmental person can help you look at whatever is creating your guilt feelings, whether they be acts, thoughts or some perceived omissions. Another person's rationality can help you evaluate your guilt and keep you from overemphasizing the negative.[2]

If you are resilient, you find your guilt diminishing over a period of time. When the guilt creeps in you're able to evict it more quickly each time it occurs. Whenever guilt becomes a part of your life, the following questions may help you evaluate it. You may find help through discussing the questions with a trusted friend.

- What is the reason for the guilt I feel? Is there something I did or didn't do? If so, what was it? Would anyone else agree that I was truly responsible?
- Is what I did wrong or contrary to God's Word and teaching in any way?
- Is this something I need to make restitution for or confess to anyone?

There may be legitimate, or good, guilt in your life. Good guilt has a purpose: It shows us where we've gone wrong and what we need to change. It can motivate us to grow. This legitimate guilt (which you could experience in a crisis) happens where there is a direct cause-and-effect relationship. When this kind of guilt happens, we can do something about it. We can admit to what we've done, make restitution if necessary and above all confess it to receive God's forgiveness. Scripture shows us the feelings of a man struggling with real guilt in Psalms 51:1-12:

> Be gracious to me, O God, according to
> Thy lovingkindness;
> According to the greatness of Thy
> compassion blot out my transgressions.
> Wash me thoroughly from my iniquity,
> And cleanse me from my sin.
> For I know my transgressions,
> And my sin is ever before me.
> Against Thee, Thee only, I have sinned,
> And done what is evil in Thy sight,
> So that Thou art justified when Thou
> dost speak,
> And blameless when Thou dost judge.
>
> Behold, I was brought forth in iniquity,
> And in sin my mother conceived me.
> Behold, Thou dost desire truth in the
> innermost being,
> And in the hidden part Thou wilt make
> me know wisdom.

> Purify me with hyssop, and I shall be clean;
> Wash me, and I shall be whiter than snow.
> Make me to hear joy and gladness,
> Let the bones which Thou hast broken rejoice.
> Hide Thy face from my sins,
> And blot out all my iniquities.
>
> Create in me a clean heart, O God,
> And renew a steadfast spirit within me.
> Do not cast me away from Thy presence,
> And do not take Thy Holy Spirit from me.
> Restore to me the joy of Thy salvation,
> And sustain me with a willing spirit.
>
> PSALMS 51:1-12

Forgiveness belongs to us. It is always there. It can't be bought, we can't work for it. It's a gift.

> I acknowledged my sin to Thee,
> And my iniquity I did not hide;
> I said, "I will confess my transgressions
> to the Lord";
> And Thou didst forgive the guilt of my sin.
>
> PSALMS 32:5

If we confess our sins, He is faithful and righteous to forgive us our sins and to cleanse us from all unrighteousness.   1 JOHN 1:9

One of the most graphic passages about guilt is in the *Living Bible*:

There was a time when I wouldn't admit what a sinner I was. But my dishonesty made me miserable and filled my

days with frustration. All day and all night your hand
was heavy on me. My strength evaporated like water on a
sunny day until I finally admitted all my sins to you
and stopped trying to hide them. I said to myself, "I
will confess them to the Lord." And you forgave me! All my guilt is gone!

PSALMS 32:3-5, LB

Perhaps what one person wrote can encourage us to deal with our guilt.

If only I had...

treated the one I loved
more kindly.

called the doctor sooner.

understood the full extent
of the illness.

taken better care of
him or her.

not lost my temper.

expressed my affection
more frequently.

When death comes, life is
examined.

You become acutely aware of your failures, real or imagined.
You want to rectify past errors.
You wish to compensate for
the wrongs you have committed.

Some people even punish themselves
with self-destructive acts,

as if to say: "See how much I am suffering. Doesn't this
prove my great love?"

Self-recrimination becomes a way
to undo all the things that
make you now feel guilty.

And maybe you were guilty.
Perhaps you said things you
should not have said.
Perhaps you neglected to do things
you should have done.
But who hasn't?

What is past is past.
It cannot be changed.
You already have too much pain
to add to the burden of self-
accusation, self-reproach, and
self-depreciation.[3]

Fear

One of the most common emotions we experience in a crisis is fear. Perhaps
what fear does to us is best described by the following passages from God's
Word.

I heard and my inward parts trembled,
At the sound my lips quivered.
Decay enters my bones,
And in my place I tremble.
Because I must wait quietly for the day
of distress,
For the people to arise who will invade us.

HABAKKUK 3:16

Anxiety in the heart of a man weighs it down,
But a good word makes it glad. PROVERBS 12:25

All the days of the desponding and afflicted are made evil [by anxious thoughts and forebodings], but he who has a glad heart has a continual feast [regardless of circumstances]. PROVERBS 15:15, AMP

The word *fear* comes from the Old English word *faer,* which meant "sudden calamity or danger." The Hebrew word for fear can mean "dread." You probably know the sensation of all these descriptions.

Usually we can identify the source of our fears. Anxiety, however, is fear with a high level of apprehension that's not directly related to anything. And what is disturbing is when we experience these feelings without knowing why. The anxiety or fear can include numerous symptoms, such as rapid heartbeat, ringing in the ears, no appetite, upset stomach, nausea, dizziness, nightmares, tightening of the throat and difficulty in swallowing, muscle pain, poor concentration as well as memory lapses, sweaty palms and difficulty sleeping. There isn't a part of our bodies that can't be affected by anxiety.

Fear often brings along its close companion—worry. Worry is an uneasy, suffocating feeling that changes whatever we see into a mood of pessimism. It stirs up our minds and churns our stomachs. The root meaning of the word is "to choke or strangle." It's like racing the engine of a car while it's in neutral. Worry immobilizes us and causes us to focus on the worst possible situation. We ask "What if?" again and again, each time making our answer a bit worse.

Worry is like fog. Perhaps you've driven in a dense fog that wiped out all visibility from a distance of five feet and beyond. Fog has the ability to snarl the traffic of a major city and shut down an international airport. Yet a dense fog that covers seven city blocks to a depth of one hundred feet is composed of less than one glass of water.

In a similar way, a little bit of worry can fog up a lot of reality. It chills your outlook, making everything look hazy, including your perception of life. It's so easy to fall into a pattern of worry. If that's where you are right now, you're not alone.

Your feelings of anxiety are normal. You're not going crazy. Although you want to know why you're experiencing these disturbing anxious feelings and thoughts, you may not know for quite a while. Most likely you fear that the crisis that has shattered your expectations—your beliefs and your world— could happen again. The more sudden and intense the crisis event, the more fear and anxiety you may experience as a result. It will help to keep in mind that you can't explain the why of all your feelings. Also, your fear and anxiety will not always be with you. Help is available, and you will get relief.

A Resilient Response to Fear

Survivors confront their fears, identify them, put them in perspective and allow them to diminish slowly while they focus on positive improvement. Many survivors have found it helpful to list each fear and place a check by it each time it occurs. It also helps to identify what you used to fear and how you overcame it.

There's nothing that helps one to overcome fear as much as concentrating upon God's Word and committing it to memory. Dwelling on passages such as Isaiah 41:10, 43:1, Philippians 4:6-9 and Psalm 37:1-10 can create the peace you are looking for. Never avoid or give in to your fears, since each time you do so, fear grows. Face fear, admit you're fearful and then evict it.

Years ago I was privileged to meet a pastor's wife, the author of an inspiring article about a letter she wrote to her children. The letter expressed how she was once again struggling with cancer. In one part of her letter she talked about fear:

Fear has knocked at my door. Sometimes in the past five days I have let fear in for awhile. It has not been good. I have thought of silly things like: I can't wear that new spring suit we just bought on sale or that lovely wool skirt we've waited six months for. Other times I think how much I want to see Kathy graduate, go off to Bible school, fall in love with the finest

Christian man this world has ever seen, and then watch her walk down the aisle on her dad's arm. Then I think I want to see Kim married and settled. Finally, for sure, I would like grandchildren.

But, dear children of mine, these are human thoughts, and to dwell on them is not healthy. I know one of the strongest desires God has given us is the desire to live, but I want to say to God that I trust Him in this too. My vision is so limited. These human desires are the purest on earth, but if I had even a tiny glimpse of heaven I wouldn't want to stay here. Because I am human, I do. So I have decided that I will put a "No Trespassing" sign at the entrance of the path of human desires and not let my thoughts wander down it.

When fear knocks, it is my determined choice to let faith answer the door, faith that is settled on the sure promise of the Word of God.[4]

How can you accomplish this kind of settled decision? Sometimes it means asking others for help. Your fear could have a useful component to it. It could prompt you to make some necessary changes. And it could be that some of your fears have value!

A conversation I recently overheard between a man and woman illustrates the healthy respect we need to have for useful fears. This couple was discussing a life-threatening experience they faced. The man asked, "Aren't you afraid?" The woman's response was tinged with anger:

Of course, I'm afraid! What kind of person do you think I am? It isn't sensible not to be afraid when there is good reason for it. I was afraid when I was beaten as a child. I was afraid when my husband left me. I've spent a lot of my life being afraid. Show me someone who hasn't! That's why so many people resort to drugs and alcohol. It blots out their fear. There is nothing so outstanding about having fear as long as you don't act fearful— as long as you don't allow yourself to become crippled into doing nothing because of your fear. We've got to face our fear and move ahead.

Depression

When your crisis involves a major loss or disruption of your life, depression, the "common cold of the mind," begins to take over. It's to be expected. When hope is gone and the future looks bleak, despair finds fertile soil in your mind.

Losses are often at the heart of so many of the depressions of life. Any loss can trigger a reactive depression—the loss of a person, a job, a home, a car, a valued photograph, a pet. The stronger the attachment, the more intense the feelings of loss. Loss is especially devastating for women because they put so much of themselves into relationships and build strong attachments. Especially devastating are the losses of any love relationship. Maggie Scarf describes this dilemma in her classic book *Unfinished Business*:

> It is around losses of love that the clouds of despair tend to converge, hover, and darken. Important figures leaving or dying; the inability to establish another meaningful bond with a peer-partner; being forced, by a natural transition in life, to relinquish an important love tie; a marriage that is ruptured, threatening to rupture, or simply growing progressively distant; the splintering of a love affair or recognition that it is souring and will come to nothing.[5]

Often these losses lead to a crisis, but too frequently loss is not recognized as such. We're not made aware of how losses affect us. We're an ill-equipped society when it comes to understanding loss and crisis.

Are you aware that the most difficult type of loss to handle is threatened loss? Waiting for the results of a biopsy or a state bar exam, waiting to hear from the admissions office of a college to which you've applied, waiting to hear if you will be the next to lose your job in a company downsizing. Situations like these carry the possibility of loss and subsequent depression because we feel powerless to do anything about the situation.

The Old Testament story of Job illustrates in detail the role loss plays in bringing on depression. Job experienced loss to a greater degree than most of us will ever experience. He lost his wealth, his means of livelihood, his servants and his children. Eventually he lost his own physical health and sense of well-being. He experienced the depths of depression. Listen to his complaints:

> Let the day perish wherein I was born, and the night which said, "A man-child is conceived." Let that day be darkness!... Why did I not die at birth, come forth from the womb and expire?... Why is light given to him that is in misery, and life to the bitter in soul, who long for death, but it comes not, and dig for it more than for hid treasures?... For my sighing comes as my bread, and my groanings are poured out like water.... In truth I have no help in me, and any resource is driven from me.... So I am allotted months of emptiness, and nights of misery are apportioned to me. When I lie down I say, "When shall I arise?" But the night is long, and I am full of tossing till the dawn.   JOB 3:3-4,11,20-21,24; 6:13; 7:3-4, RSV

No one is immune to depression, not even a Christian. Some people will experience mild depression while others dive to the depths of despondency.

The deeper your depression the more paralyzing is your sense of helplessness. You feel passive and resigned. Everything seems out of focus. You feel as though you're in a deep, dark pit, cold and isolated. There doesn't seem to be a way out of this pit either. Depression can blind us to the realities of life. It narrows our perception of the world. We end up feeling all alone, as though no one else cares about us.

Depression affects you spiritually and can change the way you see God. A journal entry reveals one depressed person's view of God:

> It's as though I were a laboratory rat. For the rat, the walls of the maze are tall and formidable barriers; perhaps the puzzle simply cannot be mastered by the poor animal. But for the observing scientist, from his perspective, those maze walls are very small indeed and from his vantage point the solution is so obvious that he wonders why the rat is so frustrated.

> But the rat is a rat and will always be a rat. The perspective of the

scientist will never be his. He is doomed to rathood and ratness for the remainder of his rat-life. The fear and confusion he experiences, the frustration expressed in his red rat-eyes, remain uncomforted by his foggy awareness that the ever-present scientist looms over him, possessing the answers, seeing the solution, but remaining distant. The scientist has a hundred rats and if this one is stupid, clumsy or crippled—well, there are plenty of other specimens of the rat race. The data concerning poor Rat is carefully recorded in the great scientific notebook, just one rat among thousands. But to that rat, those observations are so significant because they chronicle his Everything. He has only one rat-life and that life is all he's got.[6]

It's hard to believe in a loving and personal God who knows the answers and wants us to succeed and yet seems to be far off. The psalmist reflected these feelings as well:

> O Lord, do not rebuke me in Thine anger,
> Nor chasten me in Thy wrath.
> Be gracious to me, O Lord, for I am pining away;
> Heal me, O Lord, for my bones are dismayed.
> And my soul is greatly dismayed;
> But Thou, O Lord—how long?
>
> Return, O Lord, rescue my soul;
> Save me because of Thy lovingkindness.
> For there is no mention of Thee in death;
> In Sheol who will give Thee thanks?
> I am weary with my sighing;
> Every night I make my bed swim,
> I dissolve my couch with my tears.
> My eye has wasted away with grief;
> It has become old because of all my adversaries.

Depart from me, all you who do iniquity,
For the Lord has heard the voice of my weeping.
The Lord has heard my supplication,
The Lord receives my prayer.
All my enemies shall be ashamed and greatly dismayed;
They shall turn back, they shall suddenly be ashamed.

PSALMS 6

In place of experiencing peace and joy—the light of God in your life—you feel just the opposite. You feel empty. Often Christians who are depressed feel even worse because of their false beliefs about depression. It is not a sin for a Christian to be depressed. And most of our depression is not brought on by sin.

Many people are surprised to read the account of Jesus' depression in the Garden of Gethsemane. Jesus was a perfect man and free from all sin, yet complete in His humanity and tempted as we are. Look at the account in Matthew 26:36-38, AMP:

Then Jesus went with them to a place called Gethsemane, and He told His disciples, "Sit down here while I go over yonder and pray." And taking with Him Peter and the two sons of Zebedee, He began to show grief and distress of mind and was deeply depressed. Then He said to them, "My soul is very sad and deeply grieved, so that I am almost dying of sorrow. Stay here and keep awake and keep watch with Me."

Jesus knew what was about to happen to Him and it caused Him to be depressed. He did not feel guilty over being depressed and neither should we. But our depression creates a distortion of life and intensifies any guilt feelings we have. Thus, guilt over depression leads to more depression.

If you tend toward depression, even before experiencing a crisis, then your depression will be intensified during a crisis.

A Resilient Response to Depression

Listen to your depression. There's a message in it. It's telling you that something is amiss in your life. It's like a warning system or a protective device that can keep you from further stress. Admit your feelings to another person who can help you. Don't believe the messages your depression is telling you, for depression heavily distorts toward the negative. Be aware that depression immobilizes you and makes you feel lethargic. You actually begin to behave in a way that will reinforce your depression. You will need to counter your feelings and do the opposite of what your feelings tell you. You may be able to do this by yourself and you may not.

Listen to what Jane learned about her depression:

I've struggled with this depression for ten months now. My divorce, along with the demotion at work, crushed me. Through counseling and reading I finally got to the place where I could accept my depression as normal and didn't feel guilty over it. One day I sat down and tried to figure out what my depression was trying to say to me. It dawned on me that the depression was a symptom and there were causes. I began to list them. The two losses helped to bring on my depression. So did the fact that I was rejected by my husband and at work. I realized I was eating more to help me feel better but it made me not like myself. So I made some plans with some friends to hold me accountable. I'm learning to grieve my losses and say good-bye to some dreams. I've learned that since I was rejected I started to reject myself. I'm no longer doing that! And I've changed my food habits. The depression is still around, but I see it lifting. Now I have the hope that someday it will leave.

If feelings of lethargy and depression have settled over you like a fog, learn as much as you can about depression. Read about it. Discover its meaning for your life. Consider what you have been through recently. Your depression is just a part of the normal array of feelings you may need to experience as you move on to recovery. Above all, keep focused on the strength of the Lord and His Word.

Those who survive are people with faith, especially faith in the promises of God. Dwell on His promises. Believe them:

Blessed are those who mourn, for they will be comforted.

MATTHEW 5:4

Come to Me, all you who are weary and heavy-laden, and I will give you rest.
MATTHEW 11:28

Blessed be the God and Father of our Lord Jesus Christ, the Father of mercies and God of all comfort; who comforts us in all our affliction.

2 CORINTHIANS 1:3-4

When you pass through the waters, I will be with you; and through the rivers, they will not overflow you. When you walk through the fire, you will not be scorched, nor will the flame burn you.
ISAIAH 43:2

And in the same way the Spirit also helps our weakness; for we do not know how to pray as we should, but the Spirit Himself intercedes for us with groanings too deep for words.
ROMANS 8:26

For I am convinced that neither death, nor life, nor angels, nor principalities, nor things present, nor things to come, nor powers, nor height, nor depth, nor any other created thing, shall be able to separate us from the love of God, which is in Christ Jesus our Lord.
ROMANS 8:38-39

My grace is sufficient for you, for power is perfected in weakness.

2 CORINTHIANS 12:9

For Thou dost light my lamp;
The Lord my God illumines my darkness.
PSALMS 18:28

The Lord is my light and my salvation;
Whom shall I fear?
The Lord is the defense of my life;
Whom shall I dread?   PSALMS 27:1

Perhaps the best way to deal with emotions that invade your life is to follow the example of a hiker who had just read the Forest Service instructions of what to do when you encounter wild animals, especially mountain lions. This man was jogging with his dog and came upon a mountain lion. The lion began to stalk the man and then ran after him. Fortunately, the man remembered what he had read. So he stopped, turned around and faced the mountain lion. The lion was not expecting this, so it stopped and walked away. Your emotions are like that mountain lion. Face them head-on, listen to their message and eventually you will rise above them.

When we go through a crisis, we sometimes believe that God has abandoned us. He hasn't.

When we go through a crisis, we sometimes feel as if nothing matters. There are things that matter.

When we go through a crisis we sometimes think life is not worth living. It is!

In times of loss and sorrow we people of faith have to "believe against the grain." In our weakness, God reveals His strength, and we can do more than we thought possible.

Faith means clinging to God in spite of our circumstances. It means following Him when we can't see Him. It means being faithful to Him when we don't feel like it.

Resilient people have a creed that says, "I believe!" and they affirm this creed daily. In essence they say:

- I believe God's promises are true.
- I believe heaven is real.
- I believe God will see me through.
- I believe nothing can separate me from God's love.
- I believe God has work for me to do.

"Believing against the grain" means having a survivalist attitude. Not only can we survive a crisis, but out of it we can create something good.[7]

Suggested Reading

When Anger Hits Home, by Gary Oliver and H. Norman Wright, Moody.

Good Women Get Angry, by Gary Oliver and H. Norman Wright, Servant.

Why Worry? Conquering a Common Inclination, by James R. Beck and David T. Moore, Baker.

Afraid No More, by H. Norman Wright, Tyndale.

Dark Clouds, Silver Linings, by Dr. Archibald D. Hart, Focus on the Family.

Coping with Depression, by Siang-Yang Tan and John Ortberg, Baker.

FIVE

— ◆ —

"Who Am I Now?"

Adjusting to the Loss of a Family Member

The loss of significant people in our lives is inevitable. We will all face such loss sometime. Often the loss happens suddenly and traumatically. At other times the loss is expected. Either way, it creates a tremendous sense of crisis and sometimes a significant loss of identity.

Since 1988 I've lost three cousins, two uncles, a sister-in-law, my mother and my son. When the loss is a highly significant person, we feel pain, and nothing and no one can prepare us for the extent of that pain. Has anyone told you what to expect when you lose your parents, a sibling, a child or a friend? I doubt it. But most of us will experience such loss. We grieve when a major loss like this occurs. We call it "grief work" because grieving is work.

When you lose a significant person you will not only grieve over the person you have lost but over the wishes, needs, hopes, dreams and unfulfilled expectations you had for them. You may also grieve not just for your present loss but for what you have lost in the future. Perhaps there was something you never had in your relationship with the person, and now you realize you will never have it. I've worked with numerous women who didn't have a good relationship with their father. When he died, that shut the door on any hope they had for reconciliation.

This chapter cannot tell you all you need to know about grieving over the loss of significant people in your life. But it will alert you to concerns and issues that most people have never considered. Knowing this will help give you the resilience you need. (At the conclusion of this book is a list of guidelines and steps to take in your grieving process.)

When you lose a significant person in a sudden, unexpected death, you are at high risk for a pattern of complicated grieving. Sometimes the grief response evolves to a condition known as Post Traumatic Stress Disorder (PTSD), which you will read about in a later chapter. Why does this happen? Consider the cumulative effect of the following factors when your capacity to cope crumbles.

- Your assumptions about control, predictability and security are lost.
- Your loss makes no sense whatsoever.
- It's difficult to recognize the loss.
- You can't even say good-bye or finish any unfinished business.
- Your emotional reactions are heightened much more than when a natural death occurs.
- Your symptoms of grief and shock persist, which demoralizes you.
- You may tend to hold yourself responsible more than you normally would.
- You experience a profound loss of security and confidence in your world. In fact, you're shattered.
- You tend to focus on the negative aspects of the relationship with the deceased, rather than having a balanced view.
- You have sudden major secondary losses because of the unexpectedness of the loss.

All of these factors could lead you to experience PTSD.[1]

The day I was writing this I heard the news report about the Delta plane in Pensacola, Florida. An engine blew apart as it was taxiing down the runway and parts penetrated the cabin of the plane, killing a mother and her twelve-year-old son. This was a tragedy so out of the ordinary and devastating that many who were touched by it could be traumatized for life. Certainly the remaining family members will be struggling with it for years, but so will the other passengers on the plane, especially those who sat in close proximity to the mother and son.

As you recover from such a significant crisis or loss, at times you will be ambushed by grief. There's no other way to describe it. Some call it a "grief spasm," an onslaught of grief that hits you suddenly when you least expect it. You may choke up or cry, your chest may feel constricted and a wave of sadness overwhelm you. This is a normal response, but you need to stop everything else when it happens and deal with your feelings.[2]

The Tasks of Grief

As you grieve you endeavor to come to the place where you can accept and live with the loss of a significant person in a healthy way.

To be resilient in grief you need to learn how to function without this person in your life. You won't have the interactions and validation you were used to experiencing with that person. The loss of their physical presence in your life means that your needs, hopes, dreams, expectations, feelings and thoughts will change. Slowly, over time, the reality of separation begins to sink in and you realize, "For now, I exist without this person as a part of my life."

When you lose a person, you may discover it will take time to identify all the ways this person was a part of your life. It's a step-by-step process. The loss of companionship, how much you depended upon the person, how much you relied on his or her opinions—all of these are new and separate losses that make up the major loss of your life.

Each time you start to respond to the person who is no longer there, you discover again that he or she is gone. It's a fact, and there will be many reminders. You may automatically turn to the person to take care of a task he or she usually handled for you only to realize anew that the person is gone.

Whenever someone is gone from your life, you have to *broaden your roles and your skills* and learn to function without the person. You learn to make up for what you have lost. You change what you do, take over new responsibilities and find another person to help. There will be some things you don't do anymore. Adjustment necessitates not behaving the same way you did when the person was a part of your world. (This is also true when you lose a significant activity in your life through job loss, expulsion from school, loss of a house and so on.)

Moving Beyond Grief

Getting on with your life involves several steps, some of which may come as a surprise to you. Few people are aware of these steps before they experience a major loss.

Some people either resist these steps or become stuck in their grief work. Sometimes after people have gone through these stages they are able to sit down and identify what they have experienced. But what a difference it can make in your life if you're aware of the process at the time you're going through it. The awareness doesn't necessarily lessen the pain, but it gives you a direction and lets you know you're on track and not going crazy. These steps apply to the more serious kind of losses.

One of the first things you must do is *develop a new relationship* with the person you lost. You have to untie the ties that connected you to this person. The change involves keeping the loved one alive in your memory in a healthy and appropriate manner.

Formation of a new identity without this person's presence in your life is another step. As one person said, "That portion of my life is history. I will never be that way or be that person again."

Most couples who marry dream of growing old together. But when the crisis of death occurs, there is not only the loss of that dream but many secondary losses as well. Hopes, wishes, fantasies, feelings, expectations and the needs that you had for that person are gone.

There's a loss in the future as well. Your identity is now that of a widow or widower, a single person rather than a married one. When a wife loses her husband she loses someone with whom she would have shared retirement, birthdays, the bed, church functions, children and grandchildren, weddings. Look at all the roles a spouse fulfills, and what is lost when he or she dies.

friend	parent
handyperson	protector
lover	organizer
gardener	provider

companion	cook
sports partner	bill payer
checkbook balancer	laundry person
mechanic	confidant
encourager	mentor
motivator	prayer partner
business partner	source of inspiration or insight
errand person	teacher
tax preparer	counselor
child	

As you walk through these steps and do your grief work, the emotional energy once invested in the person you lost is now freed up and reinvested in other people, activities and hopes that in turn can give emotional satisfaction back to you.

Death ends a loved one's life but not your relationship with that person. How do you develop a new relationship with the person you have lost? This is not a morbid or pathological process. It is a very normal response. Yet, have you ever heard a discussion about such a relationship? Does anyone openly talk about it? Probably not. If people tell you that the best way to deal with your loss is to forget the person, they are inhibiting your grief experience.

We keep people alive all the time as we reflect upon who they were, their achievements and their impact upon us and society. I've heard a number of people say, "I wonder what he would think if he were alive today," or, "Wouldn't she be surprised to see all of this!"

It helps to be with others who have experienced the same type of loss, for they can assist you in the process of adjusting to your new identity.

How Long Will I Feel This Way?

How long does it take to recover and complete your mourning? Much longer than most people believe. The amount of time can vary, depending upon many factors.

It's been said that the average length of mourning is approximately two years for a natural death. In the case of a terminally ill individual, the time following the death could be less, since much of the grieving happened prior to the death.

The unanticipated nature of accidental death can be a major factor in contributing to a grief reaction that lasts for several years. One study indicated that the majority of mourners who experienced the loss of a spouse or child in an automobile accident were still dealing with the death in thoughts, memories and feelings four to seven years afterward.[3]

No one can tell you how long your grief will last. Grief has a beginning, a middle and an end. But many get stuck in the middle, and most don't understand the dynamics and duration of grief. This makes it even more difficult to adjust.

The emotional upheaval associated with bereavement includes a number of common elements: a sense of yearning and searching, a sensitivity to stimuli, feelings of anger, guilt, ambiguity, impatience, and restlessness, and a strong need to test what is real. As we can see from this chart, these feelings intensify and fade in peaks and valleys.

Intensity Phases of Bereavement

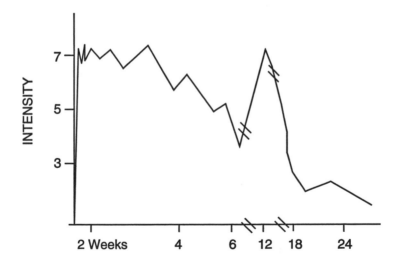

Notice the jagged peaks. The pain and grief actually intensify at three months and then gradually subside, but not steadily. They go up and down. Most people experience a rush of grief and pain at the first-year anniversary of the loss of a loved one that rivals the initial feelings. If anyone tries to tell you that you should be "over it by now" or "feeling better" at any of those peak times, you may become quite upset. That's understandable. It's also understandable that people don't appreciate the grief process unless they've been through it themselves.[4]

Time after time when I've shown this chart in seminars, people have come up and said, "Why didn't someone warn me about the three-month and one-year anniversary? It would have made it easier to handle. I thought I was going crazy!" Another problem is that most people feel that after three months of grieving a person ought to be doing all right.[5] So they pull their support away at a time when the one in grief needs it more than ever.

Death of a Parent

The first death I ever experienced with a family member came when I was twenty-two. My father was killed in a traffic accident driving home from work. He was seventy-two. What I remember was the devastating news and shock. When my mother died in 1993 at the age of ninety-three, it was a loss but not a shock. Her illness was gradual, and she had wanted to go home to be with the Lord for several years.

When Dad died, there was a sense of missing out on future events, especially since my wife and I discovered the week after the accident that we were going to be parents. Losing the first parent can often be a lingering pain as you constantly witness the effects of this loss on the remaining parent. And you can feel added pressure as you feel responsible in a new way for helping the remaining parent.

When you lose a parent you lose a person who for many years has been the most influential person in your life. For most of us, losing a parent means losing someone who loved us and cared for us in a way no one else does or ever will again. We can no longer gain their approval, praise or permission. Feelings of attachment to a parent are unique.

When parents die you lose your direct link to the past as well as to parts of yourself you may have forgotten. Not only that, you're much more aware of your own immortality. You feel more vulnerable because your parents aren't there to buffer life's ups and downs. When the second parent dies, it's like the last chapter of a book. For some it means they can never go home again, psychologically or physically. When you have to close up your parents' home and sort through what is left, you experience an abundance of secondary losses.

As you grow older, you often become attached to your parent in a new way. Now it's more of an adult-to-adult or friend-to-friend relationship. I've seen the closeness of my wife and her mother. The roles have reversed from the parent caring for the child to the child caring for the parent. And when Joyce's mother dies, even though she's in her nineties and wants the Lord to take her, it will be very painful for Joyce.

Responses to the death of a parent vary from person to person, depending on the quality of the relationship. If you've had a good relationship with a parent, you wish it could continue. You feel let down now that your parent has been taken away. For others, the loss is also the loss of opportunity to make up for difficulties in the past. You may feel cheated that you lost out on doing more for your parent(s).

For some there may be a sense of relief. The fear that you would someday lose your parents was a reality, and now you plan to go on with your life.

Perhaps the person to whom you were closest wasn't a birth parent. It may have been an aunt or uncle or even a surrogate parent. It's important that you face what you are feeling with this loss, experience the fullness of the grief and all the secondary losses and then move forward in your life without the person.

Not everyone has a good relationship with his or her parents. This can complicate the grief response. In some cases I've seen a person express relief over the death of a parent. At last he or she feels a freedom from conflict and pain. For many it's a new chance on life, an opportunity not to have to try to please someone they could never please. You may feel relief from demands you've struggled with for years. Or you may feel relief because your parent died of a lingering terminal illness that made it difficult to take care of them as well as drained your finances.

As you grieve the loss of a parent, keep in mind that other family members will grieve differently because of the quality of their relationships with the parent. Your siblings, spouse and children had a different relationship than you did.

When your parents are gone, who takes their place or continues their role? Perhaps they were the peacekeepers for all the children and grandchildren. Who does that now? Perhaps they orchestrated the family get-togethers. Who takes on that role now? Decisions concerning home and property must be made and family heirlooms divided up. The passing of parents will definitely affect your relationship with your siblings.[6] Consideration of some of these changes in advance makes it easier for the surviving member.

Death of a Sibling

One of the least talked about losses in adulthood is the death of a sibling. And if you come from a large family, you could experience more sibling deaths than other losses. There seems to be an unspoken expectation that a brother or sister's death will have very little impact upon a person. It's true there are many variables to affect your response to a sibling's death. But let's assume you were raised with this sibling and experienced normal sibling involvement.

Losing a sibling means losing someone who was a part of your significant memories, both pleasant and unpleasant. Your sibling has been in your life as long or almost as long as your parents. His or her death can make you feel older. Someone who knew you in a unique way is gone. And if he or she was the last family member left except for you, you may begin to think about when and how you may die.

You could feel a sense of responsibility for your sibling's spouse and children. Previous trips to see them were probably based more upon seeing your brother or sister. Now that your sibling is gone, you may wonder what your role is. You may worry about losing contact to some degree. If your sibling was the favorite child or the most recognized, you may wonder whether you will assume that role and whether you would receive the same response when you die.

Death of a Marriage

There are other types of losses you may encounter in your life or in the lives of other family members. Your own marriage may remain intact throughout your lifetime, but that may not be the case for others in your family. Divorce is always a shock, but especially when it happens to your own children or even to your parents. Divorce turns your life, your dreams and your ideals upside down.

I spoke with parents who had experienced the divorce of all three of their adult children. In one case, their daughter and three children came to live with them for a year. Their adult son needed financial help, and his ex-wife moved two thousand miles away with the children. The parents' retirement and travel plans went out the window as they became involved in helping their children pull their lives back together.

When your parents divorce, it can be devastating. Much is said and written about the impact of divorce on children and adolescents. But what happens when you are in your twenties or thirties and you discover that your parents are divorcing? As one married daughter said,

When they told me they were divorcing after thirty-nine years of marriage, I felt like I'd been run over by a truck. Why them? Why now? I had this image of a huge building collapsing and sending its debris in every direction. For the next few weeks I walked around in a fog. My parents! I didn't know what to do or say. We'd never be together again for the holidays. Why did they do this? Didn't they know they were disrupting all of their kids' lives?

Other Family Losses

A divorce impacts your social life, your family traditions, your life at school and at church, your economy. Its losses multiply, and all too often family members take sides. Crisis? Often the family just moves from one crisis to another. Grieving? It can go on forever and there may never be any closure.

There are some family losses that are less acknowledged and lack public rituals of support, even though they impact all family members. Consider runaway or missing children or those missing in a war. A mother shared with me that her son was in the Army and went to the Gulf War. He never came home. He was just "missing." No word. No closure.

You can be missing a family member when they are absent from the family, but they can also be missing when they are physically present. Such situations as workaholism or alcoholism in a family member create an emotional hole in the fabric of the entire family.

Terminal or Chronic Illness

Serious illnesses don't impact just the one who is ill; they affect everyone around the ill person. Chronic illness has been likened to an octopus that reaches out and grasps everyone within reach of its tentacles and holds them for as long as the effects of the illness continue. It's also unpredictable, like a terrorist who demands everything from you that you value most—your energy, money, time, stability, peace of mind and dreams for the future.

Many illnesses are unpredictable and constantly changing. This keeps caregivers in a state of upset as well. Some illnesses begin with a sudden crisis, remain chronic and finally end in death. And all this time the lives of other family members are disrupted as they attempt to carry on a somewhat normal life while caring for the sick person.

Recently I received a letter from a friend of mine. For years he was active in ministry, first as a pastor and then as director of a national ministry. For the past several years most of his time has been divided between ministering and caring for his wife as she has struggled with cancer. She has gone from surgery to surgery, from remission to remission. The treatment caused hair loss as well as weight loss.

The current letter told of her breaking both legs, having a fistula, or break, in the bowel and finally a colostomy. He talked about the details of the daily care and the support group of faithful friends and family. He described his own ups and downs as well as concerns over his wife's dying. He shared his feelings of exhaustion, loss, loneliness, uselessness and guilt. He never expected this to be a part of his life. None of us do. He survived because of his faith, his ministry to others and a strong support network of family and friends.

Health issues can become a permanent way of life for an estimated 14 percent of the population. This number increases to 25 percent of those between the ages of forty-six and sixty-five and 45 percent of those older than sixty-five.

When an illness is chronic, such as coma, dementia or Alzheimer's, the loss has a sense of ambiguity. You know your loved one is going to die but you don't know when. Some families have been known to shut out physically present family members long before they die. They do this for self-protection and survival because they can't tolerate death or a lingering illness. The greater the sense of not knowing the outcome, the greater the sense of helplessness a person feels.

When a serious illness strikes, identity and family roles need to change. When family members are able to accept the reality of what is occurring and make these changes, they are able to function more effectively.

A diagnosis that strikes fear into anyone who hears it is, "You have Alzheimer's." Estimates indicate there are close to three million Alzheimer's victims at the present time. Unless we find a way to prevent its onset this number will increase to close to ten million in the next thirty-five years.

Alzheimer's has been called the disease of the century, not just for what it does to the victim but for the devastation it causes the victim's family and friends. Some families become powerless as they try to care for the victim. If the victim is elderly, the caregiving spouse can become an "invisible patient," succumbing to a variety of diseases often brought on by around-the-clock care. The family members experience one loss after another as they watch the progression of this disease.[7]

Ken Gire describes his visit to the small town where he spent his boyhood. He meandered around town and then went to visit his aunt, his last remaining relative there. His description of the visit captures what it is like to live with Alzheimer's.

Now Alzheimer's.

That was the worst, I think. Forgetting not simply where you put your glasses or car keys, but forgetting where you've been and where you are, forgetting who you are and once were, whom you loved and who loved you.

Her husband and daughter wheeled her into the other room and lifted her into bed. When they returned, we talked about her condition and what doctors were doing for her or not doing, what medication she was taking and how she was reacting to it, what kind of diet she was on, things like that. She couldn't do anything for herself. Couldn't dress herself, feed herself, bathe herself. She was like a baby, only a baby that weighed something like ninety pounds, which made dressing her and bathing her and putting her to bed an exhausting ordeal. Her babbling was like a baby's, too, except at times the tone was insistent, even angry. She was declining fast and would have to be put in a nursing home, they told me.

When time came for me to leave, I went into the bedroom to say my last good-bye to an aunt who all of her life had loved me but who now no longer even knew me.

I touched her hand and stroked the soft, slack skin on her arm. "I have to leave now," I told her, trying to get her attention over the babbling. And as I reached down to hug her, the babbling stopped. "I love you," I said, as I kissed her forehead. Her frail, slack arms reached up to me, trembling with weakness, and she tried the best she could to hug me and said, "I love you too."

She remembered who I was. Maybe only for a moment, but she remembered.

As I got into my car, tears pooled in my eyes. So this is how it all ends. This is how we slip out of this world, with all the limitations of a baby but with none of its loveliness. Every day losing a little bit of our motor skills and a little bit of our minds. Every day losing more of our balance and losing more control of our bowels. Every day losing a little something else until at last there's little else to lose except life itself.[8]

As long as a person lives like Ken's aunt, there is suffering. This disease is just one of many that some will have to face. Loss and family members go hand in hand. This is life. So it's better to be aware of the possibility of such losses and prepare for the unexpected, especially the uninvited.

Just remember that along with the pain of loss there can be growth. We will be different. Pain offers an opportunity to "grow into the likeness of Christ." It can produce maturity in our lives if we let it.

Moreover let us also be full of joy now! Let us exult and triumph in our troubles and rejoice in our sufferings, knowing that pressure and affliction and hardship produce patient and unswerving endurance. And endurance (fortitude) develops maturity of character, (approved faith and tried integrity). And character [of this sort] produces [the habit of] joyful and confident hope of eternal salvation.   ROMANS 5:3-4, AMP

SIX

— ◆ —

The Ultimate Bereavement

Surviving the Death of a Child

The death of a child is unlike any other loss. It's a horrendous shock, no matter how it happens.

Years ago, when infectious diseases ran wild, child death was common. Today that has changed, and most deaths occur naturally and expectedly among the elderly. Our society is prepared for death with this group, and we handle it relatively well. But the pain of grieving over a child is intense, complicated and seems to linger forever.

Loss Through Infertility

Many couples have grieved over their inability to have children. So many hopes and dreams have been crushed by the inability to conceive, yet too often there is little or no social recognition for this loss, and the couple has to endure the insensitive comments of others. This loss affects the entire direction of a person's life. Listen to the words of one woman who struggled with infertility.

It was a rainy summer afternoon five years ago when I boldly put it to the Lord, "I need more of You if I am going to live wholeheartedly as a Christian. I feel dry and in need of a major shift. You need to intervene,

Lord. Do you hear me?" I marked that moment in my mind, knowing I was truly in earnest. Then I waited for more of God.

And God began to answer me in a way I did not at first recognize.

My husband and I could hardly wait to have children. We had recently bought a home and readied our lives for the little ones we dreamed of having. As months passed, a tragic truth began to reveal itself. We were unable to conceive a child.

If you have not struggled with infertility or walked with someone who has, you may be quite unaware of the level of sorrow and pain that accompanies it. For women who long to have children, it is a life-shaking event of significant loss that leaves an indelible scar on their lives. Infertility is a very real grief.

My husband and I spent a great deal of time trying everything medically possible within our moral and ethical framework to conceive a child. Infertility treatment is arduous, invasive, stressful and expensive—a roller coaster of soaring hopes and deep disappointment. At the end of all of our efforts, we were unable to bring a child into the world.

Adoption had been brewing in our thoughts, and soon we began to work in earnest to adopt a child. Little did we know that we had begun another journey fraught with perils. Many potential adoptions came our way, but each one failed. Some came ever so close to success, and we were minutes from holding our long-awaited child, when one of the biological parents suddenly had a change of heart. The process began to seem like a very cruel trick that we had to fall for again and again.

Where was God in all this? In the midst of the years of struggle and stress, I spent a great deal of time "in God's face." As Christians we believe that God can intervene on our behalf whenever he wills to do so. We had prayed and we had worked, and now there was nothing left to do but to pray. I poured out my sadness to the Lord, searched for meaning, dreamed about possible endings that would bring sense to this great struggle, and called out to him daily for help.

I prayed on the doctor's table. I prayed when I could not sleep. I prayed in the car on the way to finalize an adoption and on the way home through tears when it had failed. I prayed during the long idle periods of waiting when no adoption was in sight. And finally, I learned to pray that if God did not plan to give us a child, would he please then give us more of Himself to fill our emptiness.

In C.S. Lewis' children's book *The Lion, the Witch, and the Wardrobe,* there is a scene in which one of the main characters, a young girl named Lucy, first encounters Aslan, the great lion who is the Christ figure in this book. Lucy sees Aslan and exclaims with trepidation to one of the talking animals, "Is he safe?" The animal responds, "Safe…? Who said anything about being safe? 'Course he isn't safe. But he's good. He's the King, I tell you." This came to my mind many times. When we give our lives to God, we must receive all that comes our way from his sovereign hand. All that we face is an opportunity to surrender, to release our control, to lie prone for radical surgery as he carves out more room for himself in our lives. He is not safe, not predictable, not shallow, not obedient to our commands. But he is good.

The Lord did not leave me alone trying to hold on to his goodness. He gave me a stalwart husband who is an optimist by nature and a loving friend. God gave me dear friends and family who spoke for him and assured me of God's work, his care, and his plan. These people grieved with me but kept pulling me up to the truths of who God is. His character became much more real to me; it became essential to my interpretation of life.

Then the unimaginable happened. I became pregnant. At the same time, a baby girl became available for adoption, but our agency did not want us to adopt if we were pregnant; so with regret we let this little one go. As the weeks turned into months, I began to heal from the sorrows of the past and embrace this most wonderful gift of life. I worried something bad might happen, but I told the Lord that I could not handle a miscarriage. I told him this would be testing me beyond what I could endure. I entrusted him with this little life and let go of my fear.

My husband and I visited the doctor for our thirteenth week ultrasound and anticipated seeing our baby. We were excited, but as the doctor viewed the screen, his countenance clouded. He could not find a heartbeat. Gently he told us that our baby had died. My worst nightmare had become reality.

God's sovereignty seemed to me then like a jagged cliff from which I had been thrown. Now I was free-falling without any sense of where I would land. I was disoriented spiritually and emotionally, devastated, confused, appalled, and furious.

Two passages of Scripture came to my mind frequently during the first few days of grief. "… Rachel weeping for her children; and she refused to be comforted, because they were no more" (Matthew 2:18). I understood that kind of weeping. I also reflected on Isaiah 53 that speaks of Jesus as a man of sorrows and acquainted with grief. He was smitten, afflicted, bruised and crushed. God in his sovereign wisdom allowed his Son to experience the deepest human sorrows and afflictions in order to draw near to us. And it dawned on me that I was now in fellowship with his sufferings.

God has a reputation of coming to men and women in the darkness of night. He announced Christ's birth to the shepherds at night, brought the children of Israel out of the bondage at night, called to Samuel and opened the jail cell of Paul and Silas during the night. Night covered the earth when Jesus, our Atonement, breathed his last. God works in the darkness of our lives. It's where we should look for him.

The summer following my miscarriage felt like the summer from hell. I vacillated between feeling as if God had carelessly crushed me under his foot and as if he must have some incredible purpose that I could not yet see. I struggled between tremendous anger with God and a longing to trust him.

Again, Christian brothers and sisters listened as I tried to make sense of the loss. My husband loved me through all the dark days that seemed to have no end. God's ways and character were almost always the subjects of my thoughts.

I had a prayer stuck on my refrigerator it seemed for years. It became *my* prayer. I hope it can also be yours:

"O Lord, by all thy dealings with us, whether in joy or pain, of light or darkness, let us be brought to thee. Let us value no treatment of thy grace simply because it makes us happy or because it makes us sad, because it gives us or denies us what we want; but may all that thou sendest us bring us to thee, that, knowing thy perfectness, we may be sure in every disappointment that thou art still enlightening us, and in every enforced idleness that thou art still using us; yea, in every death that thou art still giving us life, as in his death thou didst give life to thy Son, our Savior, Jesus Christ. Amen"[1]

After reading her letter I wanted to know more about what helped her and her husband to survive. When we talked later she said, "It was my *family* and *friends*. There was a group of people around to *encourage us*. I asked them to help me by not letting me *retreat* into a shell inside of myself. At times I wanted to—especially around other women who were expecting. But *I was open* about what had happened and basically I educated others. *I reached outward* rather than inward. I was also *sympathetic* toward others who didn't understand and made comments that weren't helpful or supportive. No one had ever educated them on what to say. I also found that it helped me to *reach out and help others* who were experiencing the same problem I was.

"What really helped sustain me was the women's *Bible study* I attended. It was an in-depth study that helped me focus on who God is, his character and how he works. I also *listened* to Christian music and *meditated* on what I heard" (italics added for emphasis).

Did you notice what she did to make her a survivor?

Loss Through Miscarriage and Stillbirth

The death of a child through miscarriage is not recognized much in our society. Yet up to 25 percent of all pregnancies end in miscarriage. In many cases there may not have been any external signs of the pregnancy. Few people may have known about it. For those other than the parents, the child wasn't yet real.

It doesn't matter how long a mother carries her child. The intensity of the parents' grief response will be determined by the hopes, expectations and the meaning this child had for them. In most cases it takes six to nine months for the woman to recover emotionally from a miscarriage. Even though the child wasn't born yet, emotional bonding with the child occurs.

All the experiences and symptoms of normal grief are experienced in the wake of a miscarriage. Women, especially, may experience feelings of worthlessness, failure and deficiency. But it's not just the grief over this loss, it's the possibility of losses in the future. What if there can be no more conceptions? What if there's another miscarriage? What if this is a pattern? Who's at fault? And then there's the companion emotion—guilt. Again, especially on the part of the woman, her cry is, "I must have done something to cause this!" Or as another writer describes the process:

The questions are varied and many, depending on your individual circumstances. As you continue to review the pregnancy and birth, you define the boundaries of what you perceive as having been your personal responsibility. You release some of the guilt and begin the long, slow process of fully acknowledging your loss. As long as guilt is the major issue, the baby cannot be relinquished. The baby is held on to with "If onlys." If only I hadn't run ... or stayed up the night before ... or eaten too much ... or cried too much ... or taken a diuretic ... and on and on.

Along with the guilt you inflict on yourself is the guilt you either assume or imagine coming from other people. For example, some husbands intentionally or inadvertently insinuate the child's life was in the wife's domain, thereby implying she should have prevented the death. Even the idle remarks of relatives or friends can reinforce existing guilt or produce new guilts. The father who says, "I told you to quit smoking!"; the sister who self-righteously proclaims, "My doctor told me not to drink at all during pregnancy, and I didn't"; the neighbor who asks, "Weren't you still going to work in your eighth month?" adds to your self-blame.[2]

Many people feel it is helpful to actually see the results of the miscarriage in order to fully experience the impact and help the grieving process. Others keep the ultrasound pictures (if any were taken), which helps to make the loss real. Both steps help to confirm the loss which is an important step in recovering.[3]

Recently my wife and I received the following announcement in the mail reflecting a miscarriage loss:

Brian and Carrie
sadly announce the birth and death
of their daughter,
Emily Jo Buckalew
on May 25, 1996 at 12:39 P.M.
weight 2 lb. 10 oz. length 16-1/2 in.
We will love her always.

On the back side, the parents said:

Dear Friend,

Acknowledgment of our baby's short life may be upsetting to you. You may think the less said the better. Until now we did not know how important it would be for us to tell you of our little baby, even though our baby died. You can help us through this difficult time by letting us talk about our sorrow when we feel the need, allowing us to cry when we want, and not pretending everything is okay ... when it's not. It will take time, but with your support we will make it.

Everyone who received the card realized the significance of the loss and was invited to reach out and support the couple.

It is not abnormal for the parents to experience an intensity of grief on anniversaries of the child's death or what would have been the child's birthday.

A Glitch in the Life Cycle

One of the most difficult and disturbing issues to handle is the wrongness of a child's death. It just shouldn't happen. It doesn't make sense. It's death out of turn. The parents often feel, "Why should I survive when our child, who should have survived us, didn't?" Death violates the cycle that children grow up and replace the old.

When you lose a child, you also lose what your child represented to you. You feel victimized in so many ways. You feel as though you've lost part of yourself. The child's features and characteristics that bore resemblance to you or your spouse hit the hardest.

You will miss the physical interaction as well as the sight, sound, smell, and touch of your child. If you were still in the hands-on caregiving stage with your child, this absence will be terribly painful.

Your child embodied your connection to the future, and that no longer exists. If your child was old enough to respond to you, you've lost a very special love source. That love was based on need, dependence, admiration and appreciation. Now it's gone. You've lost some of your own treasured qualities and talents as well, for you saw some of those qualities that you value most in your child. Further, you've lost the expectations and dreams you had for your child as he or she grew older. The anticipated years, full of so many special events, have been ripped from you. If this was an only child and there is no opportunity to have another, the loss puts an end to your family line and influence in the world. There is no one else left to carry it on.

You may also see your child's death as a failure on your part. You feel anger and frustration because you were unable to exert some control over what happened to your child.[4]

Dr. Therese Rando graphically describes this feeling:

With the death of your child you have failed in the basic function of parenthood: taking care of the children and the family. You are supposed to protect and provide for your child. You are supposed to keep her from all harm. She should be the one who grows up healthy to bury you.

When you "fail" at this, when your child dies, you may feel that you have failed at your most basic function.

The death of any child is a monumental assault on your sense of identity. Because you cannot carry out your role of preserving your child, you may experience an oppressive sense of failure, a loss of power and ability, and a deep sense of being violated. Disillusionment, emptiness, and insecurity may follow, all of which stem from a diminished sense of self. And this can lead to the guilt which is such a common feature in parental grief.[5]

Because of all these losses, your grief over the death of a child will be more intense and last longer than grief over the loss of any other person significant to you. The death of a child has been called the ultimate bereavement. You need to accept this and let others know about it as well.

You will continually struggle with anger at what happened, anger at anyone you feel could have prevented it, at the unfairness of what transpired, at the disruption of your life and at God. The anger will come and go for years.

As a bereaved parent, you'll have to "grow up with the loss." Parents tend to mark their lives by the events involving the accomplishments of their children. The dates when those events would have occurred will still come around, even though your child won't be there to experience them. The sixth birthday; the first teen birthday; the times when your child would have received a driver's license, graduated, married, had children; all will bring a resurgence of your grief when you least expect it.

Our son Matthew died at the age of twenty-two. He was a profoundly mentally retarded child and at his death was about eighteen months old mentally. He lived in our home until he was eleven and then lived at Salem Christian Home in Ontario, California. At the age of twenty-one he developed a condition known as reflux esophagitis, a burning of the lining of the esophagus. He was given medication, but after that didn't work, Matthew went into the hospital for corrective surgery. Following the surgery, complications and infection set in. After a week had passed, additional surgery was performed.

My wife Joyce tells what happened next in her own words:

As I visited each day, our time together was special. I patted Matthew's hand and talked to him in simple, loving words. He didn't reach out and respond, but his eyes followed me as I moved about the room. It was touching to see him content and peaceful, even during his times of discomfort.

I was aware of God's presence through the days at the hospital. I was reassured that He was in control, and I had a sense of being uplifted by the prayers of family and friends. I was even able to reach out to a family dealing with their son's tragic motorcycle accident, which had caused massive trauma to his head.

After a week, additional surgery was performed. Following the operation, Matthew stayed in the intensive care unit. He was heavily sedated and unconscious. There were eight tubes in him, and he was constantly on a ventilator. He developed adult respiratory disorder syndrome. We were hopeful when the fever dropped and his blood pressure stabilized, but in several days we could see that he was not responding. The doctors felt he was in the Lord's hands. We prayed at his bedside for the Lord's will to be done.

We had stayed at our home the night of March 14 instead of at a motel near the Loma Linda Hospital. I woke up at 4:00 A.M. with the feeling that Matthew was worse. I called the hospital, and the staff confirmed my fears. They had gone to full power on the ventilator. Around 7:00 that morning, as we were getting ready for the day, we received a phone call. It was one of the medical staff, and he said, "We would like you to come to the hospital as soon as possible." His request didn't need any amplification.

Fortunately, we were able to speed through the traffic those sixty miles to the hospital. Both of us were aware that it could be Matthew's final hour. We had not seen any response from him for days.

Norm and I walked into the room, and the doctors told us that Matthew's lungs and heart were failing and would probably stop in about an hour. My initial response, which might surprise you if you've never had a loved one suffer and die, was profound joy. I was truly happy for him. I said, "Oh, he'll be in the presence of the Lord this day!" I knew he would be finished with the struggles of this world, totally healed and finally out of pain.

We both felt that way. But we also felt helpless since there was nothing anyone could do to make Matthew well again. As much as we knew he was going to a far better place, we also knew we were facing the greatest loss of our lives.

We said good-bye to Matthew, and I prayed at his bedside, thanking the Lord for our precious child and for His provision of eternal life. As we stood there, we saw Matthew's pulse rate decline ten beats. We felt as though we were giving him back to God and saying, "He's Yours. Have Your perfect will with him." We believed God had something better for him.

Matthew's decreasing vital signs confirmed the reality that he was going to die soon. The doctors said we could stay there or wait in a family room, and we chose the latter. Within an hour, the doctors came to tell us Matthew had died. We cried and talked with them. God was truly loving and merciful when He took Matthew home that day, and we bowed to His perfect will. Perhaps others won't understand our mixture of feelings, but that's all right. We felt at peace.

Losing Matthew was a tremendous blow in and of itself. But like any major loss, it also caused a number of additional, or secondary losses. The routine we had followed for years was gone forever. We would no longer look through catalogs to select his special sleepwear. We wouldn't have the special weekends in which he would come home and stay overnight, nor would we be able to stop by Salem House to take him out to eat. Instead, we would drive past where he used to live and keep traveling along the freeway.

We faced future losses as well. Matthew would no longer be at home on Thanksgiving and Christmas, nor would we take him to Knott's Berry Farm for his birthday. Those losses we could anticipate, but each week brought others we didn't expect. (If he had been living at home, there would have been daily losses.) We couldn't call Salem anymore to see how he was doing, a topic of our conversation was gone, and certain phrases or expressions we would say to him would no longer be expressed.[6]

Even now, several years after the death of our son, Joyce and I still experience a sense of dullness or feeling down on what would have been Matthew's birthday. And when March 15 rolls around each year, we're especially sensitive, because that's when he died.

No matter how you lose a child, questions arise: "How do I recover? What steps can I take to survive?"

What can any parent do with such a loss? There is no easy way to recover. Losing a child is truly the ultimate bereavement. There are no shortcuts. You have to face your loss and let your emotions flow. God's gift of tears is more needed now than at any other time.

As you grieve, keep in mind that taking certain steps may be helpful. A major task is to break the guilt connection. The longer you let guilt linger, the more it gains a foothold and takes up permanent residence. Self-blame cripples you and your other family relationships. You may feel guilt over something you did, didn't do, thought or wished.

If others around you don't talk about the death, or seem to avoid the subject or avoid you, you may feel even more guilty, as though you did something wrong. People avoid the subject for reasons that have nothing to do with blaming you. Most people don't know what to say, and many feel anxiety over your child's death. They feel threatened. As a bereaved parent, you represent their worst fear; if it happened to your child it could happen to theirs.

Unfortunately, such a callous response leaves you without support and fails to provide the validation you need about what has happened. Nothing hurts more than being ignored.[7]

You may have to take the initiative to break the silence. When you talk about your child and what you have experienced, you let others know it's acceptable to discuss the death. If you feel you're being avoided, go to others and start conversations. Use a letter to help people know what you've been through and how they can respond to you (see chapter ten). That makes it easier to bring up the subject.

If you let others know in a loving, gentle way that you do not want to be ignored, then you will receive more care and support. Many people are concerned that talking about your loss will intensify your pain. In some of the caring cards we received after Matthew's death, people said, "I hope this letter or card hasn't increased your hurt." But even if it had brought our pain to the surface, the comfort from the card was worth it.

What are your sources of support? Look for them. Identify them. Don't withdraw, even if that's what you most feel like doing. Find a supportive person or persons and a support group. Your support people need to be accessible and available, experienced with a loss similar to yours, able to help you go on with your life and able to help with tasks and errands you are unable to do during the grieving period. (For support groups, see the list at the end of this chapter.)

As you proceed through your valley of recovery, try these three suggestions that have meant the most to me. First, *pray*. Write out your prayers in the same way that you may write out your feelings at times. Don't edit your prayers; let your feelings flow. Second, *worship*—at home and in church, as though you're the only person there. Don't worry about what others might think of your feelings and tears. Third, *read Scripture*. Let the comfort of God's Word meet your needs. Read comforting passages again and again to yourself and aloud.

In time, as other parents have, you will find meaning in what you've experienced. Listen to the words of these parents:

I really don't know why this happened to us, but I've stopped looking for the answer! I just have to put my faith in the Lord's hands.... Only He knows—only He has the answers!

The Lord works in many strange ways. At first I simply could not fathom this, but then I accepted the Lord.... He must have had His reasons, and these—whatever they are—are good enough for me.

At first I was confused and bewildered and angry. Why did this happen to us? Why did God permit this to happen...? Then I began to realize that it was the will of God.... Who am I to question further?

Nothing pacified me after Tommy's death. I couldn't understand how a loving God could allow such a thing … . However, I eventually came to realize that God was my greatest salvation; whatever His reasons are for taking Tommy, I can now accept them! I think of Him as holding Tommy in His arms until the day I can join him.

"The Lord giveth and the Lord taketh away"—that is a quote from the Bible! I never knew exactly what it meant until this thing happened … . You're right, I questioned! I was angry and filled with hate over the loss of our son … . However, the anger and hate softened as I accepted the Lord. I put myself in His hands and immediately felt a sense of peace overtake me.[8]

Again and again you will need to say good-bye to your child in many ways, perhaps for many years.

How Loss Affects a Marriage

Following the death of a child, a marriage tends to founder. It's as though the very structure of your family is under attack. You may have to intervene with your other children as they react to the loss of their brother or sister. You and your spouse may struggle with vocational pressures because of being distracted and absent from your jobs for an extended period. Daily routines seem overwhelming because of your grief, and you may pick at each other when you see things left undone. You could face a new financial burden because of the child's illness or the unbelievably high expense of a funeral. All these elements add to marital tension.

It's estimated that 90 percent of all couples who lose a child face some kind of marital struggle within the first year after the death. The divorce rate is high among couples who have lost an only child.[9] Statistics also show that in approximately 70 percent of the families where a child was killed violently, parents either separated or divorced.[10] Many marriages that dissolve were held together by a slim thread to begin with, and the child's death seemed to snap the remaining strand. It could also be that the parenting roles were more intense than the marital relationship.

However, the death of a child does not have to lead to divorce. It can become a time of mutual comfort, support and growth. Remember the story earlier of the couple who could not have children, and when the wife did conceive there was a miscarriage weeks later? I asked her, "What did the two of you do to support one another and grow through this loss?" She replied,

We talked about it. As we struggled with the infertility problem we attended conferences together and learned together. It wasn't a one-sided issue. My husband was very cooperative. That doesn't mean we always felt the same, or felt with the same intensity at the same time. I felt it was more of a tragedy than he did, but it became a tragedy for him when he realized it was a tragedy for me. He was empathetic, cooperative and supportive. We learned to do things that would be helpful for the other person and something one of us needed, even if it wasn't high on our list of priorities.

No parent is ever prepared to lose a child, regardless of the cause or the child's age. But a parent can *learn* to recover and survive through a learning process. There are no shortcuts through grief. It's painful and long, and you will wish it would go away. For a time you will live in a dark tunnel in which you're not sure if there's any light at the end. When you keep on searching for the light, you will find it. This grief lingers longer than any other, and you carry the remnants of shadow grief for years.

Ronald Knapp gives us an insightful description of such grief:

Shadow grief reveals itself more in the form of an emotional "dullness," where the person is unable to respond fully and completely to outer stimulation and where normal activity is moderately inhibited. It is characterized as a dull ache in the background of one's feelings that remains fairly constant and that, under certain circumstances and on certain occasions, comes bubbling to the surface, sometimes in the form of tears, sometimes not, but always accompanied by a feeling of sadness and a mild sense of anxiety. Shadow grief will vary in intensity depending on the person and the unique factors involved. It is more emotional for some than for others.

Where shadow grief exists, the individual can never remember the events surrounding the loss without feeling some kind of emotional reaction, regardless of how mild.

The difference between "normal" grief and "shadow" grief is similar to the difference between pneumonia and the common cold. The latter is less serious, less disruptive to life, more of a nuisance than anything else.[11]

The death of a child is something all parents hope will never happen to them. But it may. If it does happen, only God's presence and grace can help you make meaning of life once again.

A friend of mine shared a touching story of the life and death of her profoundly disabled son, Andrew, who died at the age of twenty. Perhaps this story of faith and hope will give you hope just when you need it.

The poem of "Almost Perfect" was written on Andrew's eighth birthday. Birthdays are probably one of the hardest, most depressing times, because we want to honor this child as we do the other children and yet it is very hard. There is so little response from Drew we could only guess at likes and dislikes. Certainly there are no "wish lists" to grant for him like his siblings, and gifts and celebration become meaningless.

I suppose I was feeling all of the above when I wrote this poem. If someone didn't know Andrew, the description given is one of an obedient, respectful, almost perfect child. All of the things mentioned in the poem were things I was yelling about at my other three children. So one of the biggest blessings, the most obvious blessing is that it makes me as a parent not take so much for granted of the other three's "normalcy." I have marveled at their abilities, therefore. I think all three try hard at most everything they do. All three are bright and try to bring home good grades. I am more intolerant of sibling fighting than other parents. I have put them outside at times and made them settle their disputes where I don't have to listen to them argue, much less hit one another. So my children do seem to enjoy one another. They have developed a sense of caring for others I don't see many other children displaying.

The greatest blessing in my life regarding Andrew has been a constant dependency on God. The medical field has offered no hope and little help in dealing with a handicapped child. It has been Jesus Christ who has helped me see myself as okay. Where the world shuns and cuts off, it is the church that accepts and welcomes. Where outsiders stare, comment and criticize, it is the fellowship of other Christians who weep with me and try to understand. The only hope Andrew ever had for complete recovery in life, or a new glorified body in the death of his physical existence, lay with the mercy and grace of God through the blessed intercession of Jesus, who gave His life for such as Andrew and myself. So I remain seeking to please God with my life and yearn to have a close, personal relationship with Him. I seek to understand Him through His Word—the Holy Bible. The Bible has brought so much comfort to me. Did you know that God knows every tear you have shed? Psalm 56:8 reads, "You have collected all my tears and preserved them in your bottle! You have recorded every one in your book" (TLB). Second Corinthians 1:4, 9 and 11 gives three reasons why Christians endure suffering.

"Almost Perfect" has a deeper significance to me because that is what I kept saying to the Lord as I walked and prayed with Andrew when he was only five days old. It was a "tradition" of mine that as each child was born, I realized they were only "mine" to love, care for, to raise and that they truly belonged to God from the beginning of their lives for whatever He had created them to become, fulfilling whatever purpose He, the Master Craftsman, had designed for them. Andrew was five days old when I visited a beautiful church camp in Winchester, Kentucky, and "gave him back" to the Lord, thanking Him for this precious baby boy. I kept saying how perfect he was, then I would correct myself and say, "Well, almost perfect," because only that morning the doctor had confirmed that Andrew had suffered a broken collarbone in childbirth. The medical field could do nothing for him. How minor a broken collarbone seems now compared to the life of suffering he endured.

The blessings of Andrew's life to me are too numerous to count. My life would have been so different without him. I feel I would have fallen into the same trap as most of the rest of "normal" Christian people. That being, taking God for granted, minimizing His blessings, His goodness to an ungrateful, rebellious, restless society. I don't have all the answers, but I feel they are there if we but seek His Word. John 15:15 says that Jesus has made known to us everything that the Father has made known to Him. That's a discipline to want to seek Him, to know the answers and to delve a little deeper into His words. Because Andrew lived and I am his mother, I remain dependent on the only One who can deliver us both, Jesus Christ. Because God blessed me with Andrew's life, I have learned to try to praise Him in all things and persevere.

If you have not made Jesus your personal Savior and Friend, you are missing out on the very purpose and meaning to life in its fullest sense. He died for you. He loves you just as He loved Andrew, and He's waiting with open arms to be your Redeemer, Savior, Teacher, Healer, Lord and Friend. (See John 15:12-17.)

Almost Perfect

Andrew is a good boy.
"Almost perfect," you might say.
He never talks back, never runs in the hall,
Never hits anyone.

He doesn't leave a mess behind,
Or throw toys upon the floor.
He doesn't fingerprint the windows,
Or forget to close the door.

You don't have to worry about Andrew.
He won't run into the street.
He doesn't climb trees too high,
Or ride a bike carelessly.

Andrew is very patient too.
He waits and waits and waits.
And if you say: "Stay right here, I'll be back."

He won't walk away.
You see—Andrew CAN'T.
This poem was written on June 4, 1981—Andrew's eighth birthday
by his mom, Marcia Jones.
P.S. On December 31, 1993, God rescued Andrew and
made him totally well, so now Andrew CAN!

Support Groups for the Bereaved

American Association of Suicidology
Central Office
2459 South Ash
Denver, CO 80222
(303)692-0985

The Candlelighters
Childhood Cancer Foundation
2025 Eye St., N.W., Suite 1011
Washington, DC 20006
(202)659-5136

The Compassionate Friends
Therese Goodrich, Executive Director
P.O. Box 3696
Oak Brook, IL 60522-3696
(312)990-0010

L.O.S.S.
(Loving Outreach for Survivors of Sudden Death)
13308-91 Street
Edmonton, Alberta
T5E 3P8 Canada
(403)476-7035

National Hospice Organization
1901 North Fort Meyer Drive
Suite 402
Arlington, VA 22209
(703)243-5900

National Sudden Infant Death Syndrome Foundation
8200 Professional Place, Suite 104
Landover, MD 20785
(301)459-3388

Parents Without Partners
8807 Colesville Rd.
Silver Springs, MD 20910
(301)588-9354

The Pregnancy and Infant Loss Center of Minnesota
1415 East Wayzata Blvd., Suite 22
Wayzata, MN 55391
(612)473-9372

Widowed Persons Service
American Association of Retired Persons
1909 K St., N.W.
Washington, DC 20049
(202)728-4370

Resources to Help in the Loss of a Child

I'll Hold You in Heaven, by Jack Hayford, Regal.

A Grace Disguised: How the Soul Grows through Loss, by Gerald L. Sittser, Zondervan.

Gone but Not Lost, Grieving the Death of a Child, by David W. Wierske, Baker.

I'll Love You Forever, by Joyce and Norm Wright, Focus on the Family.

SEVEN

— ◆ —

"Will My Life Ever Be the Same?"

When Time Doesn't Heal All Wounds

On Sunday morning, July 28, 1996, I read a story about Alice in the newspaper. Alice's sister had told her how beautiful the Olympic games were in Atlanta. She decided to attend and take her daughter, who had just turned fourteen.

Alice was a sales representative for a cable company and owned her own business as well. She had served in the Air Force and also as a campaign manager for many of the candidates in the Georgia House of Representatives. She was highly thought of in her neighborhood and city. When she heard there was a free concert on Friday night at the Olympics, she jumped at the chance to go.

Little did she or anyone else know that within a few days her picture would be spread across the nation in newspapers and magazines. One minute her life was full, the next minute her life was gone. She was the only person killed by the bomb that exploded in Centennial Park in downtown Atlanta. Three other people were wounded by flying shrapnel. Her daughter suffered deep wounds in an arm and leg and required surgery, but she lived. Unfortunately, she will always live with the trauma and memory of this event.

Terrorism during the Olympics. No longer does it take place only in foreign countries. We now face a new type of disruptive crisis in our lives. As one man said after he heard about Alice's death, "Of all the people they could have killed, they took just one person. Why her? Why did she have to be that one?"

Trauma

Trauma is the response to any event that shatters your safe world so that it's no longer a place of refuge. Trauma is more than a state of crisis.

Documentation of this condition goes back to the ancient Greeks and Romans. It was noted in the Middle Ages and during the Civil War in our own country. Shakespeare wrote about it in *Henry IV*. But it wasn't until World War I that the term *shell shock* was coined. Later it was called *war memories*. It came to the forefront after the Vietnam War and became known as Post-Traumatic Stress Disorder, or PTSD. It's also referred to as *trauma* or *aftershock*.

The word *trauma* comes from a Greek word that means "wound." It's a condition characterized by the phrase, "I just can't seem to get over it." This experience is not limited to those who have gone through a war. I've seen it in the mother who had one setback after another over a period of months. I've seen it in the father who saw his daughter fatally crushed in an accident years ago; in women who were sexually abused as children or who experienced an abortion. I've seen it in the paramedic, the chaplain, the nurse, the survivor of a robbery, traffic accident or rape, and in those subjected to pressure and harassment in the workplace.

If you've ever been to a rodeo, you've probably seen a rider pursuing a steer. He guides his horse next to that galloping steer and at the precise moment leaps from his horse, grabs the steer's horns and pulls it to a dusty halt. With the right amount of pressure at the right time he literally throws that steer to the ground. When you experience trauma, you are thrown about just like that steer. Your world turns wild, out of control, crazy.

What we used to see as a safe world is no longer safe. What we used to see as a predictable world is no longer predictable. If you are like most people you overestimate the likelihood that your life is going to be relatively free from major crises or traumas and you underestimate the possibility of negative events happening to you. We never dream that some things that happen to us were ever going to happen. Perhaps that's why we're so devastated when they do. What beliefs do you hold about life? What will happen to those beliefs if you experience trauma? It's important to ask yourself these questions before trauma enters your life.

If you've been living with a feeling of invulnerability, the "It can't happen to me" mentality, trauma will not only wound you and destroy this belief, it will fill your life with fear. Invulnerability is an illusion. You didn't have to be a victim of the bombing in Oklahoma City to have your vulnerability snatched away. Just viewing the vivid pictures on TV or the still photographs in the paper were sufficient to take you from the role of spectator to participant in the trauma. We all ended up feeling, "If it can happen there, it can happen here."

You see it all the time on TV. Most newscasts carry several stories with trauma potential. We see snatches of the tragedy, usually with a scene of a memorial service, a few anguished words from a family member or victim, and then the scene quickly shifts to another tragedy. It may be the last we see or hear of it, and perhaps the last we think about it. But it's not over for those involved, it's just beginning. For some the trauma will go on for years. For others it will go on forever.

What Can Lead to Traumatization?

Perhaps you're asking the question that most people ask, "How widespread are traumatic events in our country? How many people are exposed to traumatic events, such as natural and technological disasters, accidents, crime, abuse, war?" Consider this: Between the years 1967 and 1991, nearly eight thousand natural disasters were reported worldwide. These were just the *natural* disasters! These disasters killed over three million people and adversely affected almost eight hundred million.

In the United States, 75 percent of the general population has been exposed to some event that meets the criteria for becoming a trauma. The good news is that only about 25 percent of those exposed to such events become traumatized, with rape being the highest producer of trauma.[1]

You can experience a crisis and not end up traumatized. There are many people walking around today who think and feel that the state of trauma they are in is just the way life is meant to be lived. But it's not.

If you're thinking right now, "I've never been traumatized and I doubt if I ever will be," you could be right on both accounts or you could be wrong. Even if you're not the traumatized person, someone you know may be. What you understand about trauma could enable you to be a healing, supportive element in that person's life.

Physical trauma can affect a person in two ways. Obviously, some part of the body is impacted with such a powerful force that the body's natural protection, such as skin or bones, can't prevent the injury, and the body's normal, natural healing capabilities can't mend the injury without some assistance.

Perhaps not as obvious is the emotional wounding of trauma. Your psyche can be so assaulted that your beliefs about yourself and life, your will to grow, your spirit, your dignity and your sense of security are damaged. You end up feeling helpless. You can experience this to some degree in a crisis and still bounce back. In a trauma you have difficulty bouncing back because you feel depersonalized.

As the result of trauma, something happens in your brain that affects the way you process information. It affects how you interpret and store the event you experienced. In effect, it overrides your alarm system. Trauma has the power to disrupt how you process information. When you can't handle the stress, you then activate your survival techniques.[2]

Are some of us more susceptible to being traumatized than others? If I am emotionally healthy, if I came from a "healthy home," if I'm a strong Christian, will I be immune to this disorder? We are all susceptible to trauma; we are all at risk. Your previous mental stability, race, gender, level of education, previous emotional disorders or lack of emotional disorders seem to make no difference, although your ability to handle life's ordinary stresses and your personally developed coping skills can help.

What does make a difference, more than anything else, is the intensity and degree of the stress. Studies have identified fifty-eight general vulnerability factors as contributing to a person becoming traumatized. Researchers are still puzzled about which responses assist a person in adapting best to a traumatic event.[3]

If you end up traumatized, it's not because of a defect in you. Your personality does not alter the outcome of experiencing trauma, but trauma does impact your personality. Yes, we do vary in our responses and our capacity for endurance. Some have better coping skills than others. Those who have a strong faith in Jesus Christ and an accurate understanding of life through the Scriptures have more resources to help them cope. But for all of us there comes a point in time when our defenses are overrun.[4]

There's one last factor to consider. Those who are involved in natural catastrophes seem to experience shorter and less intense PTSD than those involved in manmade disasters. As mentioned earlier, if a natural disaster can be seen as an act of nature or God—"That's just life"—the survivors do not lose as much trust in others as those involved in a manmade disaster. Also, those who experience one trauma usually recover more quickly than those who have experienced multiple traumas.[5]

What experiences qualify to create trauma in our lives? There are a multitude of events. As you read the list, consider the people you know, including yourself, who may have experienced such natural catastrophes as earthquakes, fires, floods, hurricanes, tornadoes, volcanic eruptions, landslides or life-threatening windstorms. I've been in threatening windstorms and been jolted out of bed by earthquakes. As a teen my family's life was saved by our collie barking and alerting us to a fire in our home. None of these events were severe enough to traumatize me.

Sometimes there are community or work-related disasters, such as a chemical spill or explosion.

Trauma can occur in the survivors of a refugee or concentration camp.

Many people have become traumatized through sexual or physical assault, and some have gone through satanic ritual abuse.

Children who were physically mistreated by excessive beatings, spankings, confinement or deprivation of food or medical care can be affected.

You can be traumatized by witnessing a death or serious injury in a car accident; the beating, rape, injury or death of a person in a crime; an uprising, riot or war.

The murder of a close friend or family member is traumatic. Children, who have even less capability than adults to handle significant events in their lives, can be more easily damaged. At risk is any child who has witnessed the murder, suicide, rape or beating of a family member, significant adult or friend. The number of traumatized children who experience the aftermath of gang violence in our society is growing.

Many of the conditions mentioned so far pertain to being a witness. When it happens to you, it's even worse. The list of events is extensive.

Being a combatant, prisoner or medic in a war creates the potential for trauma. Anyone who has been burglarized, robbed, mugged, abducted, raped, kidnapped or injured in a vehicular accident experiences trauma. Any situation in which you feel that you or another family member could be killed or hurt gives you cause to experience trauma.

Those involved in the helping professions are open to trauma if they've been involved in just one of the following conditions:

- witnessed death and injury;
- experienced a threat to their own safety and life;
- made life-and-death decisions;
- worked in high-stress conditions.

This last condition includes long work hours and an unsafe environment. Paramedics, rescue teams (consider the rescue workers in the burned-out hulk of the federal building in Oklahoma or the divers searching for bodies underwater amidst the torn fuselage of TWA flight 800), police officers, firefighters and medical personnel—all are at risk.

My son-in-law, who is a firefighter, received his first second-degree burns this year fighting a fire. He has witnessed numerous deaths and made many significant, life-and-death decisions. Firefighters frequently have to operate on very little sleep and sometimes work forty-eight-hour shifts.

If you or someone you know has experienced any of the above events, then you or that person has experienced trauma. This doesn't mean that PTSD or being traumatized is a result. But the *event* that sometimes leads to this problem has occurred.[6]

Keep in mind that sometimes what is traumatic to one person may not be to another.

What Happens when We're Traumatized?

Trauma has many effects. It shatters your beliefs and assumptions about life, challenges your belief that you have the ability to handle life and tears apart your belief that the world is a just and orderly place to live.

Your level of optimism begins to crumble. Even your rationality turns against you. Basically, our rationality is good and necessary. In a trauma, however, it can turn against us. Robert Hicks, in his book *Failure to Scream*, wrote:

When trauma hits, our rationality becomes a curse. We are not like an animal that, after sniffing a dead carcass, can walk off with no apparent feelings of remorse, anger or regret. Humans are more complex. We are *Homo sapiens* (Latin for "thinking man"). We think about our tragedy, and our thinking can drive us crazy. The replay of the event, the flashbacks, even the smells, bring up reminders of the trauma. As rational beings we seek the rationale in the trauma. When none is found, the traumatic blow is heightened. The meaninglessness of the event can drive one into despair, compulsive activities, abuse of substances, or addictive relationships, which are all possible quick fixes for the pain. All of these feelings illustrate the depth to which our rationality has been attacked and how shattered our world has become.[7]

We all want a reason for what happens to us. We want to know why so that we can once again have a sense of order and predictability about life. But sometimes we must live our lives with unanswered questions.

If you believe in a morality that says, "Right will always prevail and so will justice," what do you do when traumatic events that seem unfair creep into your life? What do you do when you expect the good guys to always win and the bad guys to always lose, and it doesn't turn out that way?

You won't be the first or the last to cry out against injustice. Listen to Job:

> If I cry out concerning wrong, I am not heard. If I cry aloud, there is no justice. JOB 19:7, NKJV

We want answers, we expect answers, we plead for answers, but sometimes heaven remains silent. That's when our faith undergoes a crisis in addition to whatever else is impacting us. Perhaps you end up asking along with C.S. Lewis,

> Where is God? This is one of the most disquieting symptoms. When you are happy, so happy that you have no sense of needing Him, so happy that you are tempted to feel His claims upon you as an interruption, if you remember yourself *and* turn to Him *with* gratitude and praise, you will be—or so it feels—welcomed with open arms. But go to Him when your need is desperate, when all other help is vain, and what do you find? A door slammed in your face, and the sound of bolting and double bolting on the inside. After that, silence. You may as well turn away. The longer you wait, the more emphatic the silence will become. There are no lights in the windows. It might be an empty house. Was it ever inhabited? It seemed so once. And that seemingly was as strong as this. What can this mean? Why is He so present a commander in our time of prosperity and so very absent a help in time of trouble?[8]

Trauma also affects how we see ourselves; it affects our self-identity. We all have a picture of ourselves. We may see ourselves as rational, strong, take-charge, in-control people. A trauma can change all that.

One of the main indicators that trauma may be part of a person's life is re-experiencing the trauma. Thoughts and pictures of what occurred in the form of dreams, nightmares or even flashbacks may take up residence in your life. Sometimes they slip into your mind like a video stuck on continuous replay. This sensitivity can become so extreme that an event can trigger a flashback and make you feel and act as if you were experiencing the original trauma all over again.

A friend of mine who is a Vietnam vet often experiences this at a police funeral as he sees the flag-draped coffin. I've been with those who can't watch certain movies on TV because of the effect it has on them. I've been with a person who, when the loud rumbling of a truck goes by, reacted as though it was a major earthquake hitting again, such as the one that traumatized him.

A combat veteran walks down a street and hears a car backfire. He dives behind a car to hide from the enemy and recalls the memories of his friends who were blown up in front of him. A victim of rape or sexual abuse has a flashback when making love to his or her spouse. An accident victim has a flashback at the sight of a car wreck or blood.

Reminders, or triggers, can include the anniversary of the event. As the date draws near, the intensity of the actual trauma can intensify. Holidays and other family events can create strong emotional responses. It's possible for a traumatized person to be set off by something they see, hear, smell or taste. In the case of abuse, a confrontation with the abuser may bring back emotional or physical reactions associated with the abuse.

Even the system that is designed to help the victim can cause a person to relive the painful event. It could be the court system, the police, the mental health system or the sentencing process. Certainly the media doesn't help in their graphic portrayals of the worst incidents of life, nor does the extent of violence portrayed in movies. These portrayals can bring back the memories of a traumatized person's victimization.[9]

In a flashback it's as though you leave the present and travel back in time to the original event. It seems so real. You see it, hear it and smell it. Sometimes a person begins to react as if he or she were there. Many times a person is hesitant to admit this to others for fear of their reaction. A flashback is like a cry of something that needs to come out and does so in the only way it knows how. When survivors can talk about the trauma, write about it and bring it to God in a very honest and real way through worship, there isn't as great a need for this memory to be so intrusive in nightmares, images or flashbacks.

Sometimes a person reexperiences trauma not through memories or images but through painful and angry feelings that seem to come out of nowhere. These feelings occur because they were repressed at an earlier time. Now the emotions are simply crying out for release. This state reminds me of the poem by C.S. Lewis:

> Out of the wound we pluck the shrapnel
> Thorns we squeeze out of the hand.
> Even poison forth we suck, and after the pain we ease.
>
> But images that grow within the soul have life
> Like cancer often cut, live on below the deepest of the knife
> Waiting their time to shoot at some defenseless hour
> Their poison, unimpaired, at the heart's root
>
> And, like a golden shower, unanswerably sweet,
> Bright with returning guilt, fatally in moment's time
> Defeat our brazen towers long-built;
>
> And all our former pain and all our surgeon's care
> Is lost, and all the unbearable (in vain borne once)
> Is still to bear.[10]

Perhaps you or someone you know has experienced what Lewis has described. Many have but do not realize the significance of what they are experiencing.

Another way you reexperience trauma is through numbing and avoidance. It's painful to reexperience trauma. For some, it's agonizing. They want it to go away and disappear forever, but it doesn't. And so the body and the mind take over to protect against the pain. This is done by emotional numbing. Our defense system kicks into gear to help us adjust. When numbing occurs it can create a diminished interest in all areas of life. You could feel detached from others around you, even the ones you love the most. Often there is no emotional expression because you've shut down everything. You tend to reduce your involvement with life.[11]

When you reexperience trauma, sometimes you end up feeling some of the emotion you didn't experience at the time of the event because of the numbing that took place. Now when feelings of rage, anger, guilt, anxiety, fear or sadness emerge you wonder, "Where did these come from? They hurt! I don't want them!" You shut down again so you won't feel as if you're going through a series of out-of-control mood swings. And then you begin to avoid situations you feel may trigger this condition. You retreat from other people, from family and even from life. You do this mentally, socially, physically and often spiritually.

You find yourself staying away from places where the problem occurred. If a person was robbed in a restaurant, he or she may avoid restaurants. Firefighters, police officers and medical personnel seek another line of work. A friend of mine was a counselor for a group of hospice nurses and patients. He told me he had lost forty-five people in one year who were terminally ill. He said for his own sanity he was going into another profession. It had become too much for him to handle.

People who have experienced trauma have their own set of triggers that can activate the memories of what they experienced. The effort to avoid these situations can make a person a prisoner as well as create difficulty in interpersonal relationships.

Another characteristic of trauma involves a person's increased alertness, usually referred to as hyperalertness or hyperarousal. The strong emotions you experience—fear, anxiety, anger—affect your body, particularly your adrenaline output.

When people say they are pumped up, it's usually because of an adrenaline rush that puts the body into a state of hyperalertness. Adrenaline increases blood pressure, heart rate, muscle tension, blood-sugar level and pupil dilation. Because the blood flow decreases to your arms and legs and increases to your trunk and head, you can think and move better. There's a name for this condition; it's called the "fight or flight" reaction. The fight occurs because of the increase of adrenaline. But if the adrenaline pumps in even more, you end up in the freeze response. You end up moving and thinking in slow motion. Everything seems to have shut down.

This condition is often evident by symptoms such as difficulty sleeping, periods of irritability for unknown reasons, difficulty concentrating, anxiety over crowds and being easily startled.[12]

During a traumatic event, when your heart begins to race, breathing is difficult and muscles tighten. You may label these responses as catastrophic! Some, in their attempt to make sense of what is happening to them, mislabel their bodily responses. They say, "I'm going crazy"; "I'm going to collapse"; "I'm going to have a heart attack"; "I'm dying." Some never correct the way they label these bodily responses. So anytime their heart pounds or it's hard to breathe, they misinterpret what is happening and end up with a panic attack.[13]

Sometimes emotions—like fear—feel as though a dam has collapsed and the raging waters are totally out of control. I work with many people who are paralyzed by fear. Sometimes they fear making a decision, gaining another's disapproval or taking a stand. They may fear that other people don't like them. And even worse, they fear breaking out of this pattern they are trapped in. Others are paralyzed in some other way by their trauma.

Physical paralysis is a terrible thing. To be locked up, immobilized, so that your body can't function and respond to the messages of your mind, is frustrating. But it is even more frustrating when the paralysis is the limitation or immobilization of the mind.

Scripture tells us about a man who was paralyzed in his mind (his emotions) as well as in his body:

After these things there was a feast of the Jews, and Jesus went up to Jerusalem. Now there is in Jerusalem by the sheep gate a pool, which is called in Hebrew Bethesda, having five porticos. In these lay a multitude of those who were sick, blind, lame, and withered.... And a certain man was there, who had been thirty-eight years in his sickness. When Jesus saw him lying there, and knew that he had already been a long time in that condition, He said to him, "Do you wish to get well?" The sick man answered Him, "Sir, I have no man to put me into the pool when the water is stirred up, but while I am coming, another steps down before me." Jesus said to him, "Arise, take up your pallet, and walk." And immediately the man became well, and took up his pallet and began to walk.

JOHN 5:1-9

The man in this account had been paralyzed for thirty-eight years. He lay by the pool day after day, waiting for a way to be free of his affliction. Beneath this famous pool, which was actually deep enough for people to swim in, was a subterranean stream. Every now and then the stream bubbled up and disturbed the waters of the pool. The Jewish people believed that this disturbance was caused by an angel, and the first person to get into the pool while it was bubbling would be healed from any illness.

When Jesus discovered the lame man by the pool, He asked him one of the strangest questions in all of Scripture: "Do you want to be healed?" Or to put it another way, "Do you want to change?" I suppose the man was rather taken aback by Jesus' seemingly unsympathetic question. Didn't Jesus understand that he had been brought to this pool day after day, week after week, year after year for healing? Didn't Jesus understand that he had asked person after person to help him get into the pool?

Or could it be that Jesus asked the questions because he knew what was really going on inside this man?. It's possible that after so many years of frustration in the same state of paralysis the man's helplessness had turned into hopelessness. Perhaps all hope for healing had died, and in its place was a dull despair. His answer seems to indicate this, for instead of just replying yes, he gave as an answer the reason why he could not be healed. He would go through the motions each day of trying to get into the pool, but in his heart perhaps he believed that he would never touch the water.

Many who have been traumatized feel the same way. The intensity and duration of their symptoms seems to close any door to the hope of recovery.

Three Stages of Recovery

This chapter on trauma is basic and overly simplified. The information is meant to alert you to the fact that trauma exists and is perhaps closer to you than you realize. If you identify yourself as one of those experiencing any degree of PTSD, or you know someone who fits the characteristics, remember this:

1. *Being traumatized is not incurable, recovery is possible,* but it's a slow process.
2. *You will need to work with a professional,* someone who is equipped to assist those experiencing trauma. This could include a highly trained trauma minister, chaplain or therapist.
3. *You can promote healing through understanding.* The more you learn about trauma for yourself or for others, the more you will feel in control of your life.

Aphraodite Matsakis, author of *I Can't Get Over It: A Handbook for Trauma Survivors,* has done extensive work with those suffering from PTSD. She takes a very positive approach to the healing process. For healing to occur she says you need to stop seeing yourself as a person who is diseased or deficient. It isn't you as a person who is abnormal because of your trauma symptoms, rather the event or events that you experienced are abnormal. The event was so out of the ordinary that it overwhelmed you, as it would anyone.[14]

There are three stages in trauma recovery—the *cognitive* stage, the *emotional* stage and the *mastery* stage. The cognitive stage is when you fully face your trauma, remembering it and even reconstructing it mentally. This isn't a matter of dwelling in the past but of taking fragmented and disconnected memories and pulling them together so that you can make sense of the present. Sometimes this stage involves talking with others, recreating the scene or reading any written accounts of it. When this is accomplished you will then be able to view what happened from a new perspective—an objective view rather than a judgmental view.[15]

In the *cognitive* stage you need to look at what happened to you as a detached observer (even though it may be difficult) rather than as an emotionally involved participant. If you are able to work through this stage, you will acquire a new assessment of what your real choices were during your traumatic experience. You will have a better understanding of how the event has impacted the totality of your life and be able to reduce the self-blame that most of us experience. Finally, you will gain a clearer understanding of who or what you are angry at.[16]

This stage deals with the mental area, but healing and recovery must also involve the *emotional* level. This second stage will necessitate dealing with any of the feelings you repressed in any way because of the trauma. You must experience those emotions now on the gut level. This can be difficult, because many people have a fear of feeling, as well as hurting, even worse and losing control. You don't have to act on the feelings, nor will they take over and dominate your life. But you do need to face them. These emotions could include anything from anger to anxiety to grief to fear to sadness—the list goes on and on.[17]

The final stage is the *mastery* stage. This is when you find new meaning through what you have experienced and develop a survivor perspective, rather than continue to see yourself as a victim. A person who has a relationship with Jesus Christ and a biblical worldview has the greatest potential to become a survivor.

Mastering the trauma involves making your own decisions instead of allowing experiences, memories or other people to make decisions for you. This is a time of growth, change and new direction in your life. What you learn because of a trauma you probably could not have learned any other way. Look at what Scripture says about this:

Blessed be the God and Father of our Lord Jesus Christ, the Father of mercies and God of all comfort; who comforts us in all our affliction so that we may be able to comfort those who are in any affliction with the comfort with which we ourselves are comforted by God. For just as the sufferings of Christ are ours in abundance, so also our comfort is abundant through Christ. But if we are afflicted, it is for your comfort and salvation; or if we are comforted, it is for your comfort, which is effective in the patient enduring of the same sufferings which we also suffer.

2 CORINTHIANS 1:3-6

I've had people ask me, "How do I know I'm growing and getting better?" First of all, you have to develop a new way of looking at progress. It may be slow. There may be regressions. You need to focus on the improvements rather than the times you feel stuck. One man told me that he rated his progress each month on a scale of 1 to 10, as well as his entire journey of healing at any one time. That helped him understand his own progress.

How can you tell if you're progressing and moving ahead? First of all, you can expect to see a reduction in the frequency of symptoms. In addition, the intensity of fear you struggled with over the presence of these symptoms will diminish. One of the fears that is so disheartening is the fear of going crazy or insane. This fear will also diminish.

Anger and grief, which exist hand in hand, will lessen. What remains can be directed into positive directions. Candy Lightner, whose daughter was killed by a drunk driver, founded Mothers Against Drunk Driving (MADD). A friend of mine traumatized by the Vietnam War spends time each week using his energy to help the men in our local veterans hospital. He and his Alaskan Husky take the men to the worship service and other activities. He's taught his dog to talk. I mean, people words! I've heard him, and it's amazing. He and his dog provide a great deal of entertainment and laughter. Writing letters—contacting congressmen and state senators in a properly assertive, consistent manner—does bring about change.

However, there will be times when the only way to get rid of your anger and feelings of revenge is to face the fact that you can't do anything to change what happened to you or to prevent a similar occurrence in the future. Then begin to give up a portion of your anger or resentment each day.

One victim said,

I finally realized that holding on to my anger kept me victimized. As much as I wanted someone to pay, I knew it wouldn't happen. So I decided on a ninety-day plan. I would allow myself to keep 10 percent of my anger, since I know I'm human and won't be perfect. But each day for ninety days I would give up one percent of my anger. The fact that I had a goal and then developed a plan really encouraged my recovery. Each day I spent fifteen to twenty minutes identifying who or what I wanted to avenge. I wrote it out each time and then put it in the form of a brief letter. I stood in a room and read it out loud unedited. Sometimes it wasn't pretty. And sometimes I read it to a friend because it helped having a live body there.

Each day I wrote the phrase 'I forgive you for …' and then put down the first reason I could think of for not forgiving. It was like I was full of rebuttals against forgiving. I would always end the morning by reading a praise psalm out loud. Then I would lift my hands to the Lord and give Him my anger for the day. Then I thanked Him for what He was doing, even if I didn't feel it. I discovered many things through this: I was full of bitterness. It kept me pinned down and stuck. I didn't want to forgive. They didn't deserve it.

But I kept at it. I wondered after thirty days if I'd made even 3 percent improvement. But by the time sixty days were over I felt ahead of schedule. I was improving, I was growing, I got well. Sometimes the anger and grief still hit me. I can live with that even if it's a companion the rest of my life. I have days and weeks when I feel whole again. Praise God for this.

Taking positive steps like this will help you make the shift from victim to survivor. Believing that you can become a survivor will accelerate this process.

As you move through your journey to recovery, the rigidity that helped you to cope will diminish. You will gradually discover the value of flexibility and spontaneity to the degree that you are comfortable with it, based upon your own unique personality type.

One of the delights of recovery is developing a new appreciation of life. You begin to see what you weren't seeing before, to hear what you couldn't hear before, to taste what was tasteless before.

Some people rediscover their sense of humor and all its healing properties.

You will discover a new and deeper sense of empathy for the wounded around you. In a real sense you become a wounded healer and have a greater compassion for others. The verse found in Romans 12:15, which says, "Weep with those who weep," takes on a new meaning.[18]

A common struggle in the recovery process is the ability to see and measure one's progress. For years I've had people keep a daily or weekly journal in which they explicitly write out what they are experiencing or feeling. Some keep a time-line of recovery. Some do both. What this does over time is make a person aware, in a tangible way, of his or her recovery.

A time-line recovery is a simple way to record the peaks and valleys of the recovery process. Use a monthly calendar and plot the days on the bottom with a scale of 1 to 10 on the left. At the end of each day indicate where you are for that day. This might go on for months or years, but over time you will discover that you are growing.

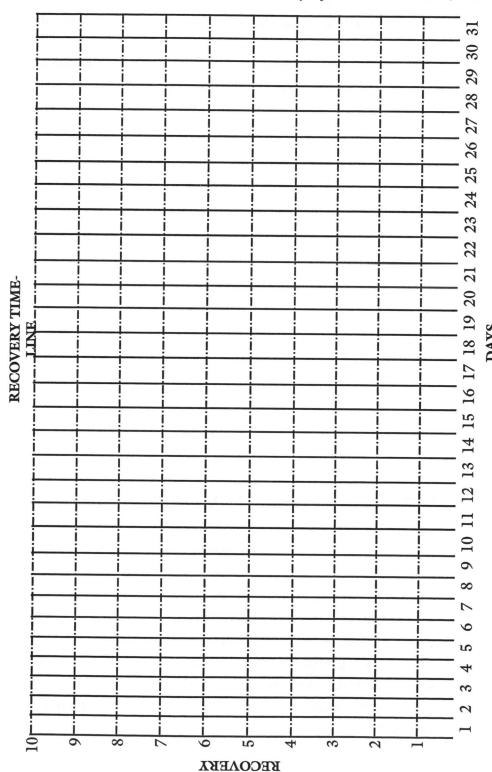

RECOVERY TIME-LINE

RECOVERY

DAYS

When you've experienced trauma, sometimes that's all you remember. What would happen if you were able to leapfrog over that event back to what your life was like before the trauma? We call this "looking at your life as it was." What was your life like? What did you do each day? Answer the following questions to help you recapture time before the trauma:

What was your biggest struggle then?

What fulfilled you?

What did you enjoy the most?

What did you look like then? (It helps to be very specific about this. Sometimes pictures and videos help the process.)

Who were your friends?

What did you like and not like about yourself?

Who did you get along with?

Who didn't you get along with?

What did you believe about God then?

What were your Christian practices, such as prayer?

What were your beliefs about life then?

What were you realistic about? naive about?

What did you want out of life then?

What were your goals or dreams for yourself then?

What are your goals or dreams for yourself now?

What would you like to be different now?

As you look at what you write, what specifically is different now? What alternatives can you come up with to make your life more the way you want it to be? Make a list of all the things you would like to have happen now (dream big) and then check off what possibly could happen if you choose to pursue this avenue. What would keep you from growing and changing? For many, it's the lack of a plan. Dreams can fade without a plan. Perhaps someone else could help you with this part of the exercise.

Overcoming trauma is a process—a journey. But you don't travel the journey alone; the Lord is with you.

The Spirit of the Sovereign Lord is on me, because the Lord has anointed me to preach good news to the poor. He has sent me to bind up the brokenhearted, to proclaim freedom for the captives and release for the prisoners.   ISAIAH 61:1, NIV

When Jesus spoke again to the people, he said, "I am the light of the world. Whoever follows me will never walk in darkness, but will have the light of life."   JOHN 8:12, NIV

You, O Lord, keep my lamp burning; my God turns my darkness into light.   PSALMS 18:28, NIV

EIGHT

— ◆ —

"God, Are You There?"

Finding God in the Midst of Suffering

God, where are you?
(Silence)
God, I'm looking for you. Where _are_ you?
(Silence)
God ... I want to know. Where are you?
(Silence)
God ... why don't you answer me?
(Silence)

God, why are you so still? Don't you care? How could you let this happen? You know what I'm talking about. Were you in Lockerbie, Scotland, when the airplane blew up? Where were you when that mother pushed her car into the lake and drowned her two sons? Were you there when that couple, who waited twelve years for that baby, buried him at fifteen months of age? Were you in Bosnia when a whole ethnic group was slaughtered? Where were you, God, when Oklahoma City happened? Were you there? Why did all those innocent children have to die?

O Lord, how long must I call for help before you will listen? I shout to you in vain; there is no answer. "Help! Murder!" I cry, but no one comes to save. Must I forever see this sin and sadness all around me?

HABAKKUK 1:2-3, TLB

Should you be silent while the wicked destroy those who are better than they?

HABAKKUK 1:13, TLB

God ... *are you there* ... you're *not* there—you're gone. I knew it. I'm abandoned.

(Silence)

God ... if you're there, all I want to know is ... why? Give me a reason. Why? Why? Why?

The psalmist cried out the same way we do:

Lord, hear my prayer! Listen to my plea! Don't turn away from me in this time of my distress. Bend down your ear and give me speedy answers, for my days disappear like smoke. My health is broken and my heart is sick; it is trampled like grass and is withered. My food is tasteless, and I have lost my appetite. I am reduced to skin and bones because of all my groaning and despair. I am like a vulture in a far-off wilderness, or like an owl alone in the desert. I lie awake, lonely as a solitary sparrow on the roof.

My enemies taunt me day after day and curse at me. I eat ashes instead of bread. My tears run down into my drink because of your anger against me, because of your wrath. For you have rejected me and thrown me out. My life is passing swiftly as the evening shadows.

PSALMS 102:1-11, TLB

Too often what we hear when we ask why is nothing—nothing at all. Why? Why? Why? The sound of silence can be deafening. Sometimes this silence comes just before something bad happens. Or right after, like the oppressive stillness after two cars finally roll to a stop after a collision heard blocks away.

As a child you heard the silence of a parent or a teacher who just stared at you after discovering your involvement in something other than what you were supposed to be doing! Or you're in a major business meeting and you speak out and contradict the chairman of the board, which no one ever does, and the silence as well as the glares are louder than thunder. Or you sit in the doctor's office and hear the silence of the doctor before he tells you a diffi-cult-to-hear diagnosis.

Nothing makes you feel more rejected than the silence of a spouse who refuses to talk with you. You feel disconnected, separated.

Often silence is the prelude to something devastating. Revelation 8:1 says: "When he opened the seventh seal, there was silence in heaven for about half an hour" (NIV).

When there is silence, you feel isolated, all by yourself, alone. As Habakkuk the prophet cried out to God, so did the psalmists.

How long, O Lord? Will you forget me forever? How long will you hide your face from me?   PSALMS 13:1 (NIV)

My soul thirsts for God, for the living God.
When can I go and meet with God?
My tears have been my food day and night,
While men say to me all day long,
"Where is your God?"   PSALMS 42:2-3 (NIV)

I say to God my Rock,
"Why have you forgotten me?
Why must I go about mourning,
oppressed by the enemy?"   PSALMS 42:9

We want answers because suffering rarely makes sense. We want answers because suffering causes us to wage a war with our beliefs. Often the biggest problem we struggle with is what we believe about problems. Dr. Lloyd Ogilvie suggests,

First of all, we believe that problems including crisis, losses and anything that doesn't go our way is bad for us. Whatever disrupts the flow of our life and is unpleasant or causes distress can't in any way be beneficial for us. Problems are a bother, an invasion, a disruption and they have no real benefit.

We also believe in entitlement. We deserve to live a problem-free life, especially if we're faithful, diligent, hard-working and plan ahead.

The third belief has to do with God. If we believe in Him, serve Him, follow His Word, He will (or ought to) make sure our life runs smoothly without any difficulty. We believe that God owes us clear sailing in life.[1]

So where is God during a crisis? He may not seem anywhere near. And if God isn't around and we can't count on Him, what hope do we have? That's the way many feel.

A pastor, Gary Kinnaman, describes what we experience:

I am sure you understand that when I speak of the absence of God, I am talking about a *sense* of absence. God is *always* present with us—we know that theologically—but there are times when he withdraws our consciousness of his presence.

In all honesty these theological niceties are of little help to us when we enter the Sahara of the heart. This is where we experience real spiritual desolation. We *feel* abandoned by friends, spouse, and God. Every hope evaporates the moment we reach for it. Every dream dies the moment we try to realize it. We question, we doubt, we struggle. Nothing helps. We pray and the words seem empty. We turn to the Bible and find it meaningless. We turn to music and it fails to move us. We seek the fellowship of other Christians and discover only backbiting, selfishness, and egoism.[2]

The biblical metaphor for these experiences of forsakenness is the desert. It is an apt image, for we do indeed feel dry, barren, parched. With the psalmist we cry out, "O my God, I cry out by day, but you do not answer, by night, and am not silent" (Ps 22:2, NIV). In fact, we begin to wonder if there's a God to answer us.

These experiences of abandonment and desertion come to us all. How, then, can we get beyond feeling abandoned? How can we know for certain that God is there with us in the midst of our suffering?

A man who struggled with cancer for twenty years wrote to a friend two years before he died:

The despair of the sufferer is not caused by the depth of the suffering but by the depth of his sense of separation from God.

You said that when you were finally able to get hold of God, the peace came. The suffering didn't diminish, it was as deep as ever, but the sense of separation had vanished. You no longer felt separated from God.[3]

How is it that we "get hold of God"?

Called to Suffer

The source for what we believe has to be the Word of God. When we look at it, we discover that time and time again Scripture tells us that God is good and He has a concern for mankind. Scripture also tells us that God is omnipotent. That means He is all-powerful. But what does all-powerful mean to you? Sometimes we look at it incorrectly. Does all-powerful mean that we are robots and He causes every single thing that happens in the world? It's true that He is all-powerful, but that doesn't necessarily mean everything that happens in the world is the way He wants it.

At the creation of the world, God created mankind with the ability to make choices. Sometimes man's choices result in things that are not what God desires. God could not give us the freedom to love Him if we didn't also have the freedom to reject Him and His teachings. He wants us to love Him based upon our own choice.

As Dr. Dwight Carlson suggests,

It is further possible that since God greatly desires individuals who willingly love, worship and follow Him, He had no alternative but to allow

Satan to test them with pain, suffering and misfortune. This is one of the major points taught in the Book of Job. Let me assure you that this does not mean God is not sovereign; in the Book of Job, Satan had to request permission to test Job, and God allowed it only within very fixed limits (Job 2:6).

Recognition of God's self-imposed limitations is the most difficult concept to grasp. Many ardent Christians will have difficulty with this viewpoint. But I am convinced that when God created the world, He set laws in motion which even He chooses to honor. The problem for us is that these laws intersect our lives in the most sensitive areas—in our suffering and our misfortune. This leads to an interesting question: Who is at the center of this universe—God or us? In his book *When Bad Things Happen to Good People*, Harold Kushner asks:

> If God can't make my sickness go away, what good is He? Who needs Him? God does not want you to be sick or crippled. He didn't make you have this problem and He doesn't want you to go on having it, but He can't make it go away. That is something which is too hard even for God. What good is He, then?[4]

This question raised by Kushner seems to reflect the idea that we are at the center of the universe and God is there to do our bidding. But C.S. Lewis has a different perspective.

> Man is not at the center. God does not exist for the sake of man. Man does not exist for his own sake.[5]

What it boils down to in this life is that you and I have been called to suffer. Suffering is inevitable.

There is another kind of suffering to which we've been called—suffering with others. And it begins first with Jesus. "If children, then heirs, heirs of God and fellow heirs with Christ, provided we *suffer with him*" (Rom 8:17, RSV). Jesus doesn't ask us to avoid suffering. He expects us to choose to suffer with Him. Why? Consider these reasons:

[God] comforts us in all our troubles, so that we can comfort those in any trouble with the comfort we ourselves have received from God.... Indeed, in our hearts we felt the sentence of death. But this happened that we might not rely on ourselves but on God, who raises the dead.... On him we have set our hope that he will continue to deliver us, as you help us by your prayers. Then many will give thanks on our behalf for the gracious favor granted us in answer to the prayers of many.

2 CORINTHIANS 1:4,9,10-11

Daniel Simundson, in *Where Is God in Our Suffering?* reminds us that:

When we cry out to God in our times of suffering, we know that we will be heard by one who truly knows what we have gone through. It is a great comfort for a sufferer to know that presence of an understanding and compassionate God, who not only invites our very human prayers but also knows what it is like to be in so much pain. God hears. God understands. God suffers with us. The lament is heard by One who has been there.[6]

God allows suffering so that we can enter into another person's sorrow and affliction. Joyce and I have experienced this numerous times as couples have sought us out either because they have a disabled child or have lost a child in death. Because we have already walked the path they are now walking, they want to talk with us.

When you experience a crisis in your life, you will have compassion and understanding for others going through the same experience. As we read in verse 11, suffering gives us the opportunity to learn to give thanks in every situation and event of life. Notice that I said "the opportunity to learn." You may not be there yet. That's all right. You'll be there someday.

Lewis Smedes puts a different light on this idea in his book, *How Can It Be All Right when Everything Is All Wrong?* (Isn't that an honest title?)

Put it as plainly as it can be put: we need to suffer some of the cussed wrongness of life in order to find its deep righteousness. We have to feel pain we do not want to feel, carry burdens we do not want to carry, put up with misery we do not want to put up with, cry tears we do not want to shed. If we feel no hurt now, we will, when all is done, be the most miserable of all people. Ultimately, at the end of the game, when we cash in our chips, it will be all right with us only if we have been hurt with life's wrongness.[7]

He suggests that there are two ways to suffer. We can suffer *from* something and we can suffer *with* someone.

We suffer from something when pain comes to us, grabs us in its claws, crushes us, unwilling, captive.

Suffering with someone does not hurt any less than suffering from something. The difference is not in the amount. The difference lies only in the will. In suffering from something, we simply receive it, nobly or meanly, with heroic courage or ordinary cowardice, but we do not choose it. In suffering with somebody, we take it into our own hands to suffer. We choose to do what we do not have to do, or even want to do; we walk, eyes open, into the pain of another human being and claim it as our own.[8]

That is our calling as believers. If you are married you will have the opportunity to suffer with your spouse. If you are a parent you will suffer with your children. You put yourself into the shoes of the other person, you experience their pain, their hurt, their agony, their burdens. It's called empathy, and it hurts. But it also has a healing quality.

We need to remember that in life, pain is inevitable, but misery is optional. We cannot avoid pain, but we can avoid joy. God has given us such immense freedom that He will allow us to be as miserable as we want to be.

Called to Rejoice

I know some people who spend their entire lives practicing being unhappy, diligently pursuing joylessness. They get more mileage from having people feel sorry for them than from choosing to live out their lives in the context of joy.

Joy is simple (not to be confused with easy). At any moment in life we have at least two options, and one of them is to choose an attitude of gratitude, a posture of grace, a commitment to joy.

Peter said, "Dear friends, do not be surprised at the painful trial you are suffering, as though something strange were happening to you. But rejoice that you participate in the sufferings of Christ, so that you may be overjoyed when his glory is revealed" (1 Pt 4:12-13). Which words leap out at you in those verses? You probably noticed the words *troubled*, *trials* and *suffering*. But remember, not only was suffering mentioned, joy was mentioned as well.

Recently I saw the musical presentation of Victor Hugo's *Les Miserables*. It's the story of grace. It's also the story of a man, Jean Valjean, who receives an unjust sentence for stealing a loaf of bread. He tries to escape and ends up spending nineteen years in jail. Both his sentence and suffering were unjust. But he also lived in an unjust world. As a result of what he experienced he became very bitter. This only intensified as he discovered what it was like to be an ex-convict in nineteenth-century France. He was constantly rejected. In time, this experience would embitter most people.

One night Valjean was so desperate that he looked for a place to stay at the home of a Catholic bishop. But Valjean took advantage of the bishop's kindness. During the night he stole most of the bishop's silver. Once again, however, he was unsuccessful in his thievery. As he tried to leave, the police caught him and took him back to the bishop's house. Much to their surprise the bishop handed two silver candlesticks to Valjean saying, "You forgot these," implying to the police that the silver was a gift.

When the police left, the bishop looked at Valjean and said, "I have bought your soul for God." And in the bishop's merciful act of claiming Valjean for God, Valjean's bitterness left him.

The rest of Victor Hugo's novel shows what happens when a life is redeemed. If anyone had a reason to hate and lash out it was Valjean. Instead he followed the bishop's example of mercy. He raised an orphan given to him by her mother as she was dying. He spared the life of the parole officer who spent years tracking him down. He saved his future son-in-law from death, even though he was almost killed in the process. He lived out the rest of his life with a sense of joy, returning good for evil.

Here was a miserable, embittered man struggling with suffering that he never deserved. But he also had another experience that was undeserved—the grace and mercy he received at the hand of the bishop.[9]

The author of *A Grace Disguised* sums it up this way:

His suffering was undeserved, but so was his redemption.

Like Valjean, I would prefer to take my chances living *in* a universe in which I get what I do not deserve—again, either way. That means that I will suffer loss, as I already have, but it also means I will receive mercy. Life will end up being far worse than it would have otherwise been; it will also end up being far better. I will have to endure the bad I do not deserve; I will also get the good I do not deserve. I dread experiencing undeserved pain, but it is worth it to me if I can also experience undeserved grace.

So, God spare us a life of fairness! To live in a world with grace is better by far than to live in a world of absolute fairness. A fair world may make life nice for us, but only as nice as we are. We may get what we deserve, but I wonder how much that is and whether or not we would really be satisfied. A world with grace will give us more than we deserve. It will give us life, even in our suffering.[10]

When We Can't Help Asking Why

When we suffer, at first we spend our energy trying to discover who or what caused our hurt and pain. In fact, most of us spend our energy trying to figure out the cause before deciding what to do with it. The more we expend our energy there, the less energy we have available to work on what to do!

Suffering and pain always produce something. Paul said, in 2 Corinthians 1:9, that pain turns us to God. Each admonition in these passages is followed by a positive result. The suffering produces something—we are changed.

This is *not* a grin-and-bear-it attitude. Nor are you to act as if nothing has happened. You are *not* in denial. It doesn't mean that you act happy and delighted about a crisis when your heart is torn apart and you feel like weeping. And it doesn't say to rejoice or be glad *immediately!* As Philip Yancey puts it:

> The Bible's spotlight is on the end result, the use God can make of suffering in our lives. Before He can produce that result, however, He first needs our commitment of trust in Him, and the process of giving Him that commitment can be described as rejoicing.[11]

Isn't it interesting that on the one hand we allow ourselves to be dependent upon Him, yet on the other hand we sabotage the comfort by making Him into a villain!

It's easy to lay the responsibility for life's tragedies upon God. Dr. Dwight Carlson writes:

> The belief that God is in control of the universe leads some people to conclude He has planned every last detail and wants every event to come about exactly as it does. Such a God would delight in pushing misfortune buttons: this God says, "Let's give Mary an 'F' on her English test today. Let's give Joanne a dent in her fender. I'll clog up Pat's sink. Joe will get a heart attack, and I'll give Susan leukemia." Nothing could be further from the truth.[12]

The other side of blaming God is believing that we are special because of our relationship with Him or because we have done something for Him, and therefore He will insulate us from the misfortunes of life.

> God might intervene—at his sovereign choosing—but it is not our divine right to demand his intervention.[13]

The problem is not with asking why, the problem is when we begin to argue with God, to demand that He defer to our demands and do it our way. If He did that, we would have created our own God.

So, we're back to the question, Why? It's a lingering question when you're in crisis. It's one you grapple with and put to bed. Then about 2:00 A.M. it jumps up and runs around again. At first, asking why is not really a question that seeks an answer. No answer would suffice, even if it were given by God. In fact, if God answered, we would probably argue with Him.

The word *why* is used again and again in the Psalms. It's a cry against that which has invaded our lives. It is a cry of protest as well as a lament. One writer said:

It places the issue of human suffering before and in front of God. It is to ask why, for what reason, to what end, does [He] remain silent? It also assumes that this suffering is unjust.[14]

Have you ever wondered what makes you keep asking this question? I mean, most of the time a part of us realizes that we won't really find an answer. But today's generation has the attitude, "We have a right to know." We need "full disclosure" of what's going on and why it's going on. Asking the why question in relationships tends to put people on the defensive, because it often has an accusatory tone or implication to it.

When our lives have been disturbed, we seem to need an answer to retrieve the orderliness we crave—there must be some logical reason for what has happened. Because most of us like order, answers and certainty, others are sometimes quick to give us glib, trite, theological answers when we're in a crisis. An unanswered "Why?" threatens the other person's security! If it happened to us, then why not to them! Perhaps this is why Job's friends responded to him as they did. And we, like Job, end up saying, "So how can you console me with your nonsense? Nothing is left of your answers but falsehood!" (Jb 21:34, NIV).

Another reason we pursue answers is to prevent the crisis from occurring again.

Perhaps we also ask in order to look outside of ourselves to diffuse our own sense of shame. We ask why to quiet the inward voice that says, "What was my responsibility in this? Could I have done more, done better, done something different so that it wouldn't have happened?" If we can find an answer outside of ourselves, we feel less guilty.

Often I think the "why" question is a way of blaming God—making Him responsible. But the real question should be, "Why *not* me?"

I've had people ask why there is so much evil in the world. But as Scott Peck observes, I've not had anyone ever ask "Why is there good in our world?"[15] I've heard people blame God; rarely have I heard them blame Satan. They blame God, but rarely do they blame the consequences of original sin.

The Benefit of Asking Why

Don't get the idea that asking why is wrong. It's a normal human response when life begins to unravel. It's the first step along the way to more significant questions and discoveries. Unfortunately, some people never progress beyond why. They remain stuck with this question for years. They never discover that it is an unanswerable question—a step toward discovering the useful questions.

Nowhere in Scripture does it tell us *not* to ask God why. Paul wasn't reprimanded because he asked God three times to remove the "thorn in his flesh." God expects us to cry out when we plow through the dark and dangerous alleys of life. It's all right to ask God to remove the present adversity. Jesus also made such a request: "Going a little farther, he fell with his face to the ground and prayed, 'My Father, if it is possible, may this cup be taken from me. Yet not as I will, but as you will'" (Mt 26:39, NIV).

James 1:3-4 talks about our response to trials. Then we read in verse 5, "If any of you lacks wisdom, he should ask God, who gives generously to all without finding fault, and it will be given to him" (NIV).

In a sense, James is saying that if you have any questions while you're going through these trials, go ahead and ask. When God believes that the answer to your question is important, He will let you know.

Moving beyond Asking Why

As Joyce and I cared for our retarded son, Matthew, over a period of time we began to ask questions. The why questions will vary for each person, but our questions took this form.

"What can we learn through this experience?"
"How can we grow through this?"
"How can God be glorified through this?"

There are no timetables or deadlines for getting beyond the why question. New questions cannot be forced, nor should they be forced upon anyone. It's a matter of growth. And asking the questions does not depend upon the problem being resolved. Sometimes you find yourself returning to the why question, even as you ask others. This too is normal.

The new questions are broader in focus and include other people. "Why?" merely focuses on self. The questions beyond why are growth questions that can prevent us from becoming stuck in the past and present. They open the door to the future.[16]

God is not obligated to explain Himself to us. Sometimes we don't have the ability to understand the reasons for a crisis, or it is impossible for us to grasp the entire picture. In several places Scripture mentions that this is the way life is:

It is the glory of God to conceal a matter.   PROVERBS 25:2, NIV

The secret things belong to the Lord our God.
                                   DEUTERONOMY 29:29, NKJV

As you do not know the path of the wind, or how the body is formed in a mother's womb, so you cannot understand the work of God, the Maker of all things.   ECCLESIASTES 11:5, NIV

"For my thoughts are not your thoughts, neither are your ways my ways," declares the LORD. "As the heavens are higher than the earth, so are my ways higher than your ways and my thoughts than your thoughts."

ISAIAH 55:8-9, NIV

We are people who usually put faith in formulas. We feel comfortable with predictability, regularity, assurance. We want God to be this way too, and so we try to create Him in the image of what we want Him to be and what we want Him to do.

However, you and I cannot predict what God will do. Paul reminds us of that in Romans 11:33, "Oh, the depth of the riches both of the wisdom and knowledge of God! How unsearchable are His judgments and His ways past finding out!" (NKJV).

God is not uncaring or busy elsewhere.

He is neither insensitive nor punitive.

He is supreme, sovereign, loving and sensitive.

Is God in control? Yes! But He's in control with infinite wisdom.

God is the absolute sovereign of the universe, but He has given us freedom. He created us to love Him, but there could be no mature love between us and Him without our freedom to choose.

I don't fully comprehend God. I, too, have unanswered questions about some of the events of my life. But all of life's trials, problems, crises and suffering occur by divine permission. As Don Baker wrote:

God allows us to suffer. This may be the only solution to the problem that we will ever receive. Nothing can touch the Christian without having first received the permission of God. If I do not accept that statement, then I really do not believe that God is sovereign—and if I do not believe in His sovereignty, then I am helpless before all the forces of heaven and hell.[17]

God allows suffering for His purposes and for His reasons. This should help us to see God as the gracious Controller of the universe. God is free to do as He desires, and He doesn't have to give us explanations or share His reasons. He doesn't owe us. He's already given us His Son and His Holy Spirit to strengthen and guide us.

We look at problems and losses and ask "Why?" Jesus asks us to look at these events and say, "Why not?" What God allows us to experience is for our growth. Just as God has arranged the seasons of nature to produce growth, He arranges the experiences of the seasons of our lives for growth. Some days bring sunshine and some bring storms. Both elements are necessary.

God knows the amount of pressure we can handle. First Corinthians 10:13 tells us that He will "not let you be tempted beyond what you can bear" (NIV). But He does let us be tempted, feel pain and experience suffering. He doesn't always give us what we think we need or want; He gives us what will produce growth.

When we ask God, "Where are You?" we may come to realize that He is always there in the midst of the crisis. But we still can't help but ask Him, "When will You answer?" just as David cried,

> How long, O Lord? Will you forget me forever?
> How long will you hide your face from me?
> How long must I wrestle with my thoughts
> and every day have sorrow in my heart?
> How long will my enemy triumph over me?   PSALMS 13:1-2, NIV

We want Him to act according to our timetable. Scripture says, "Be still before the Lord and wait patiently for him" (Ps 37:7, NIV). To block out the pain of waiting, we are often driven to frantic activity. This does not help, but resting before the Lord does:

Often waiting is a time of darkening clouds. Our skies do not lighten. Instead, everything seems to become even more grim.

Yet the darkening of our skies may forecast the dawn. It is in the gathering folds of deepening shadows that God's hidden work for us takes place.

The present, no matter how painful, is of utmost importance. Somewhere, where our eyes cannot see and our ears are unable to hear, God is. And God is at work.[18]

You may not feel that God is doing anything to help you recover. Why? Because you want recovery *now*. The instant solution philosophy of our society often invades a proper perspective of God. We complain about waiting a few weeks or days, but to God a day is as a thousand years and a thousand years as an instant. God works in hidden ways, even when you and I are totally frustrated by His apparent lack of response. We are merely unaware that He is active. Hear the words of Isaiah for people then and now:

Since ancient times no one has heard, no ear has perceived, no eye has seen any God besides you, who acts on behalf of those who wait for him. You come to the help of those who gladly do right, who remember your ways.

ISAIAH 64:4-5, NIV

God has a reason for everything He does and a timetable for when He does it:

"For I know the plans I have for you," declares the Lord, "plans to prosper you and not to harm you, plans to give you hope and a future."

JEREMIAH 29:11, NIV

Give yourself permission not to know the what, how and when of your circumstances. Even though you feel adrift on a turbulent ocean, God is holding you and knows the direction of your drift. Giving yourself permission to wait can give you hope. It is right for God to ask us to wait for weeks and months and even years. During that time, when we do not receive the answer and solution we think we need, He gives us His presence.

But I trust in you, O Lord; I say, "You are my God." My times are in your hands.   PSALMS 31-14, 15, NIV

Philip Yancey concludes his book *Where Is God When It Hurts?* with these words:

> So, where is God when it hurts?
>
> He has been there from the beginning, designing a pain system that still, in the midst of a fallen, rebellious world, bears the stamp of His genius and equips us for life on this planet.
>
> He has watched us reflect His image, carving out great works of art, launching mighty adventures, living out this earth in a mixture of pain and pleasure when the two so closely coalesce they sometimes become almost indistinguishable.
>
> He has used pain, even in its grossest forms, to teach us, asking us to let it turn us to Him. He has stooped to conquer.
>
> He has watched this rebellious planet live on, mercifully allowing the human project to continue its self-guided way.
>
> He has let us cry out and echo Job with louder and harsher fits of anger against Him, blaming Him for a world we spoiled.
>
> He has allied Himself with the poor and suffering, establishing a kingdom titled in their favor, which the rich and powerful often shun.
>
> He has promised supernatural strength to nourish our spirit, even if our physical suffering goes unrelieved.
>
> He has joined us. He has hurt and bled and cried and suffered. He has dignified for all time those who suffer by sharing their pain.
>
> He is with us now, ministering to us through His Spirit and through members of His body who are commissioned to bear us up and relieve our suffering for the sake of the head.
>
> He is waiting, gathering the armies of good. One day He will unleash them. The world will see one last explosion of pain before the full victory is ushered in. Then, He will create for us a new, incredible world. And pain shall be no more.[19]

Listen, I tell you a mystery: We will not all sleep, but we will all be changed—in a flash, in the twinkling of an eye, at the last trumpet. For the trumpet will sound, the dead will be raised imperishable, and we will be changed. For the perishable must clothe itself with the imperishable, and the mortal with immortality. When the perishable has been clothed with the imperishable, and the mortal with immortality, then the saying that is written will come true: "Death has been swallowed up in victory."

"Where, O death, is your victory?

"Where, O death, is your sting?"   1 CORINTHIANS 15:51-55, NIV

NINE

— ◆ —

Survivors, Part 1

How Do They Do It?

There are times when crisis hits that you feel like a parakeet I heard about. Everything was going along well for this little bird. His life was smooth with all of his needs met, until that fateful morning. One minute he was sitting on his perch and the next he was tumbling end over end down a narrow tube until he fell into a pile of dirt and dust.

You see, his owner had decided to clean the cage. So, she got out the vacuum cleaner and, removing the attachment from the end of the hose, stuck the hose into the cage. Just then the phone rang and with the distraction of answering the phone, she lost her grip on the hose and it settled right on the bird. Away he went.

Realizing what she had done, the bird owner dropped the phone, turned off the vacuum and fearfully opened the bag. The parakeet was alive, but stunned and filthy. She grabbed the bird, ran to the bathroom, turned on the large faucet in the bathtub and proceeded to hold him under the water. Then she realized that her bird was gasping for air, as well as shivering. So, she reached for her hair dryer, put it on high and hot air blasted him.

The parakeet? He never knew what hit him. Oh, he lived, but he never sang much after that. He just sort of sat and stared.[1] His life had been changed by an unexpected crisis.

Change is inevitable when a crisis invades your life.

What Comes after Crisis?

Crisis and change go hand in hand. The question is, do you want to be a victim of the direction change takes you, or do you want to be in charge of it? Everyone has a choice after a crisis hits. The definition of a survivor is a person (or family) who gets knocked down and stays down for the count. Then he or she gets up and does something in a different way. The nonsurvivor just gets back in the ring and gets hit all over again.

If you've already experienced a crisis, and you probably have, you know what I'm saying. Some couples and families draw closer together and become more compassionate. Others become splintered and soon disintegrate. Some individuals stagnate while other individuals grow, even as they carry wounds and scars.

Many families, instead of working out solutions for their pain and problems, begin to attack each other in the months following a crisis, whether the event is the birth of a disabled child, the discovery of a child's disability, a child's rebellion, a family member's death, a job loss. If conflicts have been buried for years, a crisis lifts the restraints, and conflicts erupt with a new source of fuel. Now the family has to deal not only with the crisis itself but with other unresolved conflicts. Each drains energy needed to cope with the other.

A family works together like a large body. Each person is an integral part of the body. When the body loses an arm (as in a death), is permanently injured (as in a disabled father), or one part refuses to cooperate with the rest and does its own thing (as in a rebellious child), all the other parts are affected. They have to learn to adjust. Sometimes they assume new roles.

It's similar to balancing an old-fashioned balance scale. If something is added to one side it alters the other side by the same amount in the opposite direction. If the scale is ever to be balanced again, something has to be added to one side or subtracted from the other.

Your family is like that scale. The members have to adjust to handle the change and get back into balance. Many aspects of family life—including power, responsibilities and roles—may need to be reassigned. The longer the central individual was in the family or the greater the significance of his or her position (such as the oldest child rebelling), the more adjustments will need to be made.

I've seen cases in which one child committed serious offenses that drew attention away from the parents' marriage problems. When the child was jailed and no longer there, the marriage problems became apparent and another child became the troublemaker to ease the marital tensions. In some families, when a parent leaves or loses a job, other issues that have gone unnoticed begin to surface.

Between the time a crisis occurs and the individual family members discover their new roles and begin to stabilize, there's a time of uncertainty and turmoil. Because of the reality of the loss, it's difficult to make some of the necessary changes. Each family member needs time and space to deal with the crisis in his or her own way. It may take a while for each one to find a new role. A person feels like a juggler at times, trying to deal with his or her own needs and still be helpful to the other family members.

After a crisis hits, you'll also have to weigh the needs of a particular family member against the needs of the family as a whole. You'll have to work to achieve a balance. What do you do, for example, when a child dies or runs away close to Christmas time? How do you respond when some of the family want to get a Christmas tree and celebrate Christmas and some don't?

How do people survive crisis? How do families survive? Must a person have a certain type of background or upbringing to be a survivor when crisis hits? Consider this:

In 1962 a fascinating report *Cradles of Eminence* was published by Victor & Mildred Goertzel. They studied 413 famous and exceptionally gifted people to learn what produced such lives. The results were not quite what a person might expect. About 80 percent of the later famous children hated school. Seven out of ten of the group came out of homes full of trauma and dysfunctions, including absentee parents, conflictual parents, poverty and a variety of physical handicaps. But almost every single handicap and difficulty had been overcome so they could become all they were meant to be.[2]

Choosing How to Handle Change

Families and individuals who cope well with heartbreak and crisis have specific characteristics, as do those who don't handle crisis well.

What sets survivors apart from nonsurvivors? There are things we can learn from the wisdom and experience of those who make it. Dr. William Mitchell suggests that nonsurvivors follow what he calls path A.

They *curse* the crisis. They add to the negative situation by adding a negative opinion. They actually compound the negativity.

They also *nurse* the crisis. Their time and attention is centered on the problem rather than on looking for a solution.

Finally, they spend their time *rehearsing* the problem. In their minds they replay it again and again until it dominates their every waking moment.

There is, however, a path B—the path survivors take. They *disperse* the crisis. One of the most effective ways of handling minor and major difficulties is to take what seems to be an overwhelming problem, break it down into smaller parts and then tackle each smaller part one at a time.

John was injured in an accident that was clearly the other driver's fault. He was incapacitated for almost a year, during which time he lost his job. After six months, disability payments ran out. The other driver was uninsured, and John's insurance was such that it barely kept pace with his medical costs. There were so many unfair aspects to this situation that it would have been easy for John to focus on the unfairness and place blame. For a brief time (one day) John and his family allowed themselves to do just that. Then they said (and these are their exact words), "We can gripe and sit on the pity pot, or we can be survivors—what will it be?"

They decided to become pioneers and carry out a new lifestyle until Dad was well enough to work. The family spent a week brainstorming how they could make do with what they had, how to cut costs to the bare minimum. They thought of ingenious and creative ways to make money and identified which friends and family members they could ask for whatever help they needed.

Since John had to stay home, he found some ways to make money there through various jobs. He also called the pastoral staff at his church to see what he could do to assist them during this time. Each week the family allowed themselves a "one-hour family gripe time" when they could dump all their feelings and complaints. Often this time turned into laughter as they learned to be "creatively ridiculous" in their griping. But they always ended their session with a time of listing their blessings and what they had to be thankful for. They concluded with a time of thankful prayers. This family not only survived a crisis, they grew through it!

Survivors *reverse* what they can about the crisis, just like John's family. This doesn't mean you can make a crisis disappear. But you can look for some glimmer of hope, some ray of light. You can choose to be problem-oriented or you can choose to be solution-oriented. You can choose not to dwell on the negative. Once again, the difference between a nonsurvivor and a survivor is in the way the person thinks about the crisis. Scripture has much to say about this.

Have this attitude in yourselves which was also in Christ Jesus.

PHILIPPIANS 2:5

Now your attitudes and thoughts must all be constantly changing for the better. EPHESIANS 4:23, TLB

Fix your thoughts on what is true and good and right. Think about things that are pure and lovely, and dwell on the fine, good things in others. Think about all you can praise God for and be glad about.

PHILIPPIANS 4:8, TLB

So watch what you do and what you think. JAMES 2:12, TLB

Let's take a more in-depth look at what makes the difference between survivors and nonsurvivors.

What Defines a Survivor?

Survivors Plan Ahead

Survivors tend to *plan ahead* in order to effectively handle the transitions of life. Losses and crises will come as unwelcome guests into every life. Survivors anticipate the possibility of future problems and make plans to handle what may happen. They make plans for coping, and they stick with their plans. They are realistic when they hear about a crisis. They are able to think about and discuss the question, "How would I (or we) handle a situation like this?"

Have you anticipated some of the difficulties you will face in the next few years? It could be anything from an unexpected move, a business failure, a death in the family, a child leaving home early or an adult child returning home. Do you have a plan for handling these "surprises"? What will you do?

One family shared with me that diabetes ran through the husband's side of the family. At this time he and three of his six siblings already had diabetes and were on insulin. Two of his siblings were not doing well, since they chose a path of denial over the years rather than face the fact that diabetes might hit them.

This family was already educating their children about the characteristics of the disease and how to identify indications that it could be creeping into their lives. The family kept abreast of the newest treatments as well as preventive approaches. Everyone carefully watched their diets, as this can be a major factor in the disease.

I've seen more and more individuals—before they are hit with a crisis—attend classes on "Handling Stress and the Crises of Life." These are people who want to prepare themselves in advance.

I live in a modest, quiet, family-oriented neighborhood in Long Beach, California. In the early nineties, following the Los Angeles riots, we experienced fire bombings, looting and rioting just three miles away. Before the final verdicts were handed down in the Rodney King police trials, the neighbors on our block met together and developed a block defense plan in case further riots broke out. We knew how to barricade our block, and we had the name of who had fire extinguishers and firearms. Who would have ever thought this would occur! We didn't want it to happen, but the possibility was strong, and we needed to be prepared.

We also live in an area plagued by fires, floods and earthquakes. A number of our friends lost just about everything in the Northridge earthquake. My mother's four houses and the home in which I was raised in the Hollywood Hills were almost destroyed by a raging fire in the late seventies, which burned twenty-five homes all around us. So the possibilities of disasters here are very real.

My wife Joyce took a "Community Disaster Training" course and participated in a simulated earthquake recovery drill. She keeps her identification vest and hard hat at hand in the closet. We also carry earthquake survival kits in each car. That's being prepared!

Individuals and families who don't do well are *not prepared* for life's setbacks. They survive well when things are going well. Some actually deny the possibility that a crisis could happen to them. When other people experience divorce, death, unemployment or illness, they seldom feel any empathy. I've actually talked with people attending my "Recovering from Loss" seminars who have difficulty identifying any major crisis in their lives.

One man said, "Norm, I just can't relate to any of these experiences people are describing. What does that say about me? Is this a problem in my life?"

I asked, "How would you handle it if you experienced some major crisis or tragedy? What would you do?"

He paused for a moment and then said, "I don't know. I've never thought about it. I guess I never thought it would happen to me."

Unfortunately, too many people believe crisis just happens to others.

Survivors Cultivate a Biblical Attitude

Some crises you know you will experience in life, but other crises take you totally by surprise.

There have been many events in or near my life that I never anticipated would happen. I never expected that an office next to mine would be blown up by a terrorist, with people injured and killed. But it happened.

I never expected a business associate to mismanage the running of my business to the extent that I would almost lose that business. But it happened.

I never expected that a high school boy on one of my outings as a youth director would fall off a four-hundred-foot cliff to his death. It happened. I watched as they carried him out in a body bag on a horse.

I never expected that my daughter at the age of twenty would take a detour in her Christian life and live with boyfriends, use cocaine and move into alcoholism. But it happened, and continued for four years.

I never expected to have my only son born profoundly mentally retarded with brain damage and then suddenly die at the age of twenty-two. But it happened.

Over the years, my wife and I have learned the truth and significance of many passages from God's Word. One passage in particular came alive as we depended on it more and more: "Consider it all joy, my brethren, when you encounter various trials, knowing that the testing [or trying] of your faith produces endurance" (Jas 1:2-3).

The Amplified version says, "But let endurance and steadfastness and patience have full play and do a thorough work, so that you may be [people] perfectly and fully developed [with no defects], lacking in nothing" (Jas 1:4).

Learning to put that attitude into practice is a process. The passage does not say "respond this way immediately." You have to feel the pain and grief first, and then you'll be able to consider it all joy.

What does the word *consider* mean? As I studied in commentaries, I discovered that it refers to an internal attitude of the heart or mind that allows the trials and circumstances of life to affect us either adversely or beneficially. Another way James 1:2 might be translated is this: "Make up your mind to regard adversity as something to welcome or be glad about."

You have the power to decide what your attitude will be. You can say about a trial, "That's terrible. Totally upsetting. That's the last thing I wanted for my life. Why did it have to happen now? Why me?"

The other way of "considering" the same difficulty is to say, "It's not what

I wanted or expected, but it's here. There are going to be some difficult times, but how can I make the best of them?" Don't ever deny the pain or hurt you might have to go through, but always ask, "What can I learn from it? How can I grow through this? How can I use it for God's glory?"

The verb tense used in the word *consider* indicates a decisiveness of action. It's not an attitude of resignation—"Well, I'll just give up. I'm stuck with this problem. That's the way life is." If you resign yourself, you will sit back and do nothing. But James 1:2 indicates you will have to go against your natural inclination to see the trial as a negative. There will be some moments when you'll have to remind yourself, "I think there's a better way of responding to this. Lord, I really want You to help me see it from a different perspective." Then your mind will shift to a more constructive response. This often takes a lot of work on your part. Discovering the truth of the verse in James and many other passages like it will enable you to develop a biblical perspective on life. And that is the ultimate survival tool.

God created us with both the capacity and the freedom to determine how we respond to the unexpected incidents life brings our way. You wish that a certain event had never occurred, but you can't change the fact that it did. The key word here is *attitude*. You can choose which attitude you will have! Listen to the story of one woman.

The day had started out rotten. I overslept and was late for work. Everything that happened at the office contributed to my nervous frenzy. By the time I reached the bus stop for my homeward trip, my stomach was one big knot.

As usual, the bus was late, and jammed. I had to stand in the aisle. As the lurching vehicle pulled me in all directions, my gloom deepened.

Then I heard a deep voice from up front boom, "Beautiful day, isn't it?" Because of the crowd I could not see that man, but I could hear him as he continued to comment on the spring scenery, calling attention to each approaching landmark. This church. That park. This cemetery. That firehouse. Soon all the passengers were gazing out the windows. The man's enthusiasm was so contagious I found myself smiling for the first time that day.

We reached my stop. Maneuvering toward the door, I got a look at our "guide": a plump figure with a black beard, wearing dark glasses and carrying a thin white cane. Incredible! He was blind!

I stepped off the bus and, suddenly, all my built-up tensions drained away. God in His wisdom had sent a blind man to help me see—to see that though there are times when things go wrong, when all seems dark and dreary, it is still a beautiful world. Humming a tune, I raced up the steps to my apartment. I couldn't wait to greet my husband with "Beautiful day, isn't it?"

—Source Unknown

As Dr. Joy Joffe puts it, "What happened to you was truly horrible. But you have a choice. You can live the rest of your life as a memorial service or you can put it away and get on with it."[3]

The 1952 Olympics were special to a young Hungarian boy. He stood in front of a target and because of his perfect right hand and eye coordination hit the target time after time. He won a gold medal in shooting for himself and for Hungary. Six months later he lost his right arm. Four years later the Olympics were in Melbourne, Australia. He was there. This time he used his left hand and he hit the bull's-eye again and again. He won another gold medal. He made a choice not to be limited by his limitations.

One of the best ways to clarify our response to what we can't understand, can't explain or do not like is set forth in a phrase by Dr. Gerald Mann. He suggests that we are "free to determine what happens to what happens to us." Did you catch that? It's a choice.[4]

Listen to the words of Tim Hansel as he fought to recover from a multitude of broken bones in his back after a fall from a mountain.

Summer 1975

I go into the hospital Monday morning again for more tests and such.
Despair.
So real.
So deep.

Paralyzed in my own pain, cynicism, and ugliness. I feel so inept, so weak, so ugly, that I want to shun even myself. I don't want to be around anyone when I'm this way, and yet I'm sure I can't solve this by myself. Everything seems like such a hassle. On days like this I feel that I've wasted most of my life.

More X-rays. More bad news. I've realized more strongly than ever that you don't truly discover your roots until you are at the bottom of the pit. From this perspective you are no longer distracted by usual superficialities which disguise themselves in masks of importance. I looked up the word *root.* It means "to dig down in some mass in order to find something valuable."

In higher orders of living things, a means of support, a reservoir of life energy. The cause, the source, the essence, the essential points or parts. The music root refers to that tone from which all other harmonies, overtones, and chords are produced. In philosophy, it is the uncompounded and uncompromised word or element without prefix, suffix, or inflectional ending. And finally, it means "to be or become firmly established, to plant or fix deeply," as in the earth. God is teaching me through all this to rediscover the substance of my strength and my song. Perhaps this is an unusual opportunity to discover who I really am.

Fall 1975

If you can't change circumstances, change the way you respond to them. It has been said that there is no such thing as a problem that doesn't have a gift in it. I'm going to have to begin to find some of those gifts and open them.[5]

When I was a child in the forties, I saw the movie *Dumbo, the Flying Elephant.* I've discovered that most people, no matter what their age, have viewed that film, thanks to video. Do you remember the story? Dumbo was a young circus elephant but a bit different from the others. He was born with huge ears. And so, the other elephants thought he was weird—a freak. The only one who didn't make fun of him, naturally, was his loving mother.

Dumbo did have his difficulties. His ears were so big that he could hardly walk without tripping on them. And he seemed to get into all sorts of trouble because of those ears. He wished he hadn't been born with this problem.

But he did have one friend. A small circus mouse felt sorry for him. He encouraged Dumbo to just ignore what others said about him and look at himself as someone special. But, it didn't seem to matter what Dumbo did, things just kept going downhill for him.

There was one scene in the film that was a turning point for Dumbo. One morning he woke and discovered that he and his mouse friend were high up in a tree nestled in the branches. They couldn't imagine how they had gotten up there. I mean, have you ever seen an elephant climb a tree? They were puzzled, and after talking about it concluded that somehow Dumbo must have flown up into the tree.

At this point in the film the little mouse said, "Dumbo, you can fly!" But it was his next statement that was so insightful. He looked at Dumbo and said, "The very things that held you down are going to carry you up and up and up."

What Dumbo initially saw as something terrible, a deformity, a limitation, became something valued. His ears didn't change, his perspective did. He found the good in what seemed to be bad.

Survivors Learn from Others

When it isn't possible to plan ahead, survivors *learn from others* who have gone through difficult times in life. Do you know someone who has survived difficulties and grown through the experience? It may be someone you know personally or someone you've read about like Joni Erickson Tada, who is paralyzed, or Dave Dravecky, the major league baseball player whose arm and shoulder were amputated in 1991 because of cancer.

In the book *Charlie's Victory*, the story is told of thirty-year-old Charlie Wedemeyer, a high school coach who was told by the doctor that he had ALS, commonly known as Lou Gehrig's disease. It's a progressive, debilitating, paralyzing disease. He was given one year to live. But for the next seven years he continued to coach.

When he could no longer walk, his wife Lucy drove him up and down the sidelines in a golf cart. In time, he couldn't talk anymore, so she read his lips and passed on his instructions to the players. In his last season after he had gone on round-the-clock life support, his team still won the state championship.

How did this man survive so long? How did this marriage stay intact? They focused on what they had together rather than on what they were missing. Lucy said,

> I think we communicate and understand each other better today than we ever did. While I've learned to read Charlie's lips, I find I often don't have to. His eyes almost always tell me exactly how he feels, and his eyebrows punctuate those feelings as they bounce up and down or his forehead furrows into a wrinkle. And if you don't think someone in difficult circumstances can find happiness and contentment, if you doubt the contagious quality of joy, well, you've never seen Charlie smile.[6]

Their commitment of love to one another made them survivors.

I have learned so much over the years in working with others in order to help them. The reality is, they help me to grow.

Survivors Express Negative Emotions in Healthy Ways

Survivors find healthy ways to *express hurt, anger* and *resentment*. They don't bottle up their hurt feelings, nor do they complain and force their discomfort on others. They talk, they share and they cry. Oh, how they cry! Tears are God's gift, especially at times like these.

When words fail, tears are the messenger. Tears are God's gift to all of us to release our feelings. When Jesus arrived in Bethany following the death of Lazarus, He wept (Jn 11:35). And so will we. Ken Gire describes the crisis of life and the value of tears.

> The closest communion with God comes, I believe, through the sacrament of tears. Just as grapes are crushed to make wine and grain to make bread, so the elements of this sacrament come from the crushing experiences of life.

And sometimes the crushing starts early.

One day your dog doesn't come home, and you go calling for it. Another day passes, and you go looking for it. And on the third day when you're looking for it, you find its stiff body on the side of a well-trafficked street, and you bundle it up, carry it off, dig a hole in the backyard, and you bury it with a rock as a tombstone and tears as a eulogy.

Or someone at school dies from a cerebral hemorrhage, or several someones in a sudden car wreck.

Or someone you've fallen in love with hasn't fallen in love with you, and you think life can't go on.

Or you learn from the orthopedic doctor that you can no longer play the sport you have loved for half of your still very young life, and maybe it's not the thing that should bring tears, but it does.

Or a grandparent dies. A grandparent who loved you and teased you and hugged you and brought "a little something for you" every time she came to visit. And now there's a freshly dug hole in the backyard of your heart.

Or a parent dies, and now the whole backyard is one big hole.

Or a marriage ends between two people you thought would be the last to break up, and besides the grief you feel, you sense the mortar of life loosening a little, and the unsettling feeling that if it could happen to them, it could happen to anyone, even to you....[7]

In a newer book, *From My Own Tears*, I have learned that if you follow your tears, you will find your heart. If you find your heart, you will find what is dear to God. And if you find what is dear to God, you will find the answers to how you should live your life.[8]

When our tears come, instead of feeling bad for shedding them, or apologizing for them, remember their value and the promise of God as stated in this poem.

Morning Will Come

Brokenhearted …
How can I bear the pain?
So many plans … permanently interrupted.
So many dreams … shattered.
Hopes … dashed.
All gone.
Why?
Why this?
Why us? Why me?
Helplessness … hopelessness …
Life will never be the same again.
Is it even worth living?
Where are you, God?
I'm right here beside you, my child.
Even though you may not feel my presence,
I'm holding you close under the shadow of my wings.
I will walk with you through this dark night.

Do not shrink from weeping.
I gave you tears for emotional release.
Don't try to hide your grief.
Let it become for you a source of healing,
A process of restoration,
For I have planned it so.
Those who mourn shall be blessed.
I'll be holding on to you,
Even when you feel you can't hold on to me.

Seek my face, child of mine.
Receive my promise, impossible as it may seem now,
That joy will come in the morning.
It may take much time,
But I will heal your broken heart.
I know the night seems endless,
But MORNING WILL COME.
I have promised.

-From The Haven of Rest Newsletter

When you don't admit your feelings, they become concealed and withheld. Bottled-up feelings lead to bitterness, vulnerability and distorted perceptions. Chaplain Robert Hicks says that in disasters those who are crying or screaming will be better off than those who sit quietly, passive, unable to let it out.

The blows of life hurt us. But often those who hurt most are silent. The screamers are better off than their silent counterparts. At least they know they are hurt and are feeling their pain. For various reasons, we don't allow ourselves to experience the pain we feel. Often others are to blame.

They don't want to hear about our pain, or it makes them feel uncomfortable about their own failure to scream, or perhaps it just makes them feel awkward. Therefore, the pain ends up being covered with work, alcohol, sex, drugs, depression, compulsive eating, dieting, and the endless list of acting-out behaviors that indicate to alert observers that all is not well. Having failed to scream, they are now screaming through their disorders, addictions, and compulsions. To scream is normal when facing tragic events. Not to scream may reveal the extent to which we are bleeding to death on the inside.[9]

Deferring the necessary noise of grief should be seen as a warning cry for an individual or a family in crisis. Unfortunately, men especially have a tendency to "go it silently alone."

Over the years, we've found that families who have difficulty coping frequently hurt one another by keeping silent. Interaction among family members is vital. Often, however, they retreat into their own inner worlds and don't express their thoughts or feelings. Sometimes some family members want to talk but others don't. The family may not communicate at critical times because they never learned to talk when everything was going well. People aren't likely to have the energy, time and capability to learn communication skills when life is falling apart around them.

Survivors Live in Community

Most people don't realize that a silent person has power over other family members. For those who want to talk, the silence adds to the pressure of the crisis, and they end up feeling rejected and isolated. *Survivors do not live independently.* They have learned to draw on their own strengths and gifts and use them effectively, yet they still ask for and can accept assistance from others. They can also express concern and warmth to others. Silence is a characteristic of dysfunctional families; it destroys and deadens hope. And as the silence progresses, estrangement and frustration increase.

Survivors Look for Solutions

Survivors concentrate more on *solutions* than on blame.

Blame is one of the most significant characteristics of individuals and families who *don't* make it. None of us likes being out of control and left hanging. There has to be some closure to discovering what created the problem in the first place. If we have an explanation for what happened, we can understand it better, handle it better and feel relieved that someone else was at fault. The more serious the crisis, the greater we feel the need to discover the cause. Statements that start with the words "If only you had/hadn't ... " or "Why didn't you/Why did you ... " begin to fly between one person and another. If a family member knows the other person's areas of vulnerability, the accusations can get vicious.

You may not want to blame others. You know that blaming doesn't make sense. But good sense doesn't often prevail after a crisis. Rather, the surge of emotional turmoil and the struggle for a reason for the difficulty becomes uppermost. When you blame you create a war zone and the other side retaliates.

Because everyone is vulnerable at this time, accusations and other comments penetrate deep into the mind and heart of the receiver and will be remembered for years. No one wants to be unfairly accused or blamed.

In the Book of Proverbs we read, "There are those who speak rashly, like the piercing of a sword" (12:18, AMP), and, "In a multitude of words transgression is not lacking" (10:19, AMP). These verses clearly reflect the pain of unfair accusation.

Perhaps it's time for you to stop and reflect on the characteristics of survivors described in this chapter. The principles stated here are helpful not just for the crisis times of life but for everyday living.

What about it? Are survivor characteristics a part of your life right now? If not, don't despair; they can be. You, as others have, can learn the steps to becoming a survivor. Like so much else in life, it's a choice. You *can* make that choice!

TEN

— ◆ —

Survivors, Part 2

How Do They Do It?

Resilience—the ability to bounce back and move forward—is what you've been reading about in this book. Some of the chapters may have been hard for you to read. That's understandable. They may have brought up memories you wish had remained buried. But resilience is not about dredging up the pain of the past; it's about equipping you for the present as well as the future.

This book is a survival guide. That's why we're looking at the characteristics of those who have survived. We can learn from the experiences of others. As you have read about some of these people, hopefully you've started to consider how to make the principles of surviving a crisis a vital part of your life. This chapter will give you even more principles.

Survivors Face Reality

Those who survive *face what has happened to them.* They don't run, avoid or deny. They name what has happened to them and face the devastation it has created. Eventually they learn to accept the existence of the crisis and its fallout in their lives and go with it instead of resisting it.

You have to face the seriousness of your crisis and the magnitude of what you have lost. You need to feel it to the depths of your soul and talk about it again and again. Sometimes people immerse themselves in a bundle of activities to avoid the pain. Activity doesn't make the pain go away. It just intensifies it.

Survivors affirm what they have lost. Going to a grave site and placing flowers is a simple way to acknowledge your loss. Joyce and I do this several times a year. Four of our family grave sites are in close proximity—Joyce's father and brother, our son Matthew and my mother.

Our country has tried to help the survivors of the Vietnam War recover by creating the Vietnam Veterans Memorial in Washington, D.C. The memorial is only visible when you walk into the grounds of the Constitutional Gardens. The piece of polished black granite starts with just one name. Then the granite grows taller and taller with row upon row of names upon it—58,022 of them. The black wall helps us to remember what we've lost. It helps the viewer focus on sacrifice, bravery, friendship and loyalty. It also helps to heal men and women's spirits.[1]

Robert Veninga summed it up so gracefully when he said, "Once you have experienced the seriousness of your loss, you will be able to experience the wonder of being alive."[2]

From his vantage point on a cliff seventy-five feet above the ocean, Wayne Monbleau learned a valuable lesson from a seagull.

I noticed a solitary seagull, slowly drifting toward me on the air currents.

In fact, quite a wind had kicked up. As it came in off the ocean, I could see the trees bending under its force. An occasional crow came scooting by, propelled forward by the strong breeze. All the while this seagull didn't seem to be moving a muscle. It just kept drifting toward me effortlessly.

Wait a minute! How could this gull be floating toward me when the wind was blowing against it? This seagull should have been riding the current away from me, not toward me. What was happening here?

My attention became completely fixed on this bird. I noticed other gulls, furiously flapping their wings as they attempted to fly into the wind. It didn't work. One by one, they gave up. They would peel off to one side, and when the stiff breeze grabbed them, they were quickly whisked away out of sight. But this single gull I had been watching for a few minutes now just kept drifting on. How long had it been since this seagull had flapped its wings? How was it able to come toward me, against the wind, while all the other birds had been exerting their full power and had failed?

As I sat there pondering these questions, I had an inner feeling that there was something important for me to see here. Then I felt the Spirit of God speak to my heart. Here is the gist of what I remember His inner voice saying to me that day: "The difference between this bird and all the other birds is that the others are fighting the wind, while this gull has learned how to submit itself to the wind. By yielding to its power, rather than resisting its power, this seagull has learned how to ride the wind. This bird has a different 'attitude.' Its body is positioned so that this contrary wind, which is beating back the others, is actually being used to propel this seagull forward. By passively accepting the breeze, this gull is going places where the others, with all their effort and straining, can never go."[3]

Survivors Don't Magnify the Problem

Families who do not cope well often magnify the seriousness of their problems. They take them to the extreme and imagine the worst possible consequences instead of being hopeful or waiting to see what the actual results will be. They interact too much and in the wrong direction. When they discuss only their crises amongst themselves, without outside objective assistance, they easily become overly pessimistic. They're not solution-oriented but problem-centered. They often use the "victim phrases" that reflect a desire to just give up.

"I can't ... "
"That's a problem."
"I'll never ... "
"That's awful!"
"Why is life this way?"
"If only ... "
"Life is a big struggle."
"What will I do?"

We hear so much today about people being victimized by someone else. But there are more people who are victimized by their own beliefs and attitudes. By using victim phrases, we reinforce the control that problems or hurts exert over our lives. Every time we think or say one of these phrases, we subconsciously begin to believe it and fulfill it. Eventually we talk ourselves into believing these phrases represent the truth, and we become victims of our own beliefs.

Survivors may start out making these statements but they learn to move from pessimism to optimism. They learn to challenge their victim thinking and come up with alternatives that will move them forward rather than keeping them stuck.

"I can't." These words are prompted by three attitudes that often hinder us from moving on with our lives—the attitudes of unbelief, fear and lack of hope.

When you say "I can't," you're saying that you have no control over your life. It's no harder to say, "It's worth a try." You'll like the results of this positive phrase much better.

"That's a problem." Those who see life's complications as problems or burdens are immersed in fear and hopelessness. Life is full of barriers and detours. But with every obstacle comes an opportunity to learn and grow if you hold the right attitude. Using other phrases, such as, "That's a challenge" or "That's an opportunity for learning something new" leaves the door open for moving ahead.

"I'll never ... " This victim phrase is the anchor of personal stagnation. It's the signal of unconditional surrender to what exists or has happened in your life. It doesn't give a person or God an opportunity to work through the crisis. It's much better to say, "I've never considered that before" or "I haven't tried it, but I'm willing to try." This opens the door to personal growth.

"That's awful." Sometimes this phrase is appropriate in view of the shocking, dire situations we often hear about or experience. In time we can learn to

respond by saying, "Let's see what we can do about this situation," or, "I wonder how I can help at this time," or, "I wonder how I can do this differently."

"Why is life this way?" This is a normal response to the deep pains and sudden shocks of life. Some people experience one hurt and disappointment after another. Others experience a major setback and choose to linger in its crippling aftermath without recovering. They continue to use this victim question over and over again for months and years. They fail to make the transition to the "what" and "how" questions—what can I learn through this and how can God be glorified through this?

Remember that life is unpredictable and unfair. It isn't always the way we want it to be. But our response to life is our choice.

Joy in life is a choice. *Growth* in life is a choice. *Change* in life can be a choice, and choice comes before joy, growth and change.

In the space of just one year one woman experienced her husband's death, a daughter's divorce and the other daughter's imprisonment. What was her response?

When pain comes, it comes in piercing, specific jolts. That's what I felt when we received a phone call that Barbara had been arrested. The pain seemed to stay in the very pit of my stomach and never left for months. It seemed to just hit in different degrees with each event that took place after her arrest. I thought then that this is the worst thing that could ever happen. I began to wonder where God was in this intense pain that wouldn't stop hurting. I spent so much time trying to figure out why we were all having to go through this before I decided how I would respond to this tragedy. I had a choice to either give up or face this head-on and trust God that He would see us through. I am glad I chose to trust my heavenly Father, because He has been faithful....

When the doctor sat across from my husband and me and told us my husband had Hodgkin's disease, the same intense pain hit me again. I thought, this is it, this was more than I could bear.

I was so afraid! Fear had taken over. How could I make it without Gary? How could I handle Barbara's situation? And Michael is only eleven years old; he needs a father. So for a year and a half I watched Gary dwindle away and each day the Lord gave me strength to take care of him and prepare me for the days ahead without him. God used all this pain in its grossest form to teach me to turn to Him and totally trust Him.

Knowing that He has hurt with me and cried with me and loved me through His Spirit and through members of His body has lifted me up. I can face tomorrow.[4]

Tim Hansel, who survived a fall in a mountain climbing accident and has been in pain for over twenty years, writes:

I've survived because I've discovered a new and different kind of joy that I never knew existed—a joy that can coexist with uncertainty and doubt, pain, confusion, and ambiguity. A journal entry a couple of years ago, written in the midst of the most trying period I've ever experienced, says simply, "I gave up looking for certainty—and found truth." I realized that when I quit waiting for certainty to come, I was free to discover, or rediscover, the essence of what I was really looking for.

Joy is a process, a journey—often muffled, sometimes detoured; a mystery in which we participate, not a product we can grasp. It grows and regenerates as we have the courage to let go and trust the process. Growth and joy are inhibited when we say "if only," enhanced when we realize that failures and difficulties are not only a critical part of the process, but are our very opportunities to grow.[5]

"If only ... " This phrase makes us into people imprisoned in lost dreams. It's possible to keep yourself bottled up with "if onlys."

There's another phrase that can release us from this and usher us into the future. The phrase "Next time" shows that we have given up our regrets, we have learned from past occurrences and are getting on with our lives.

"What will I do?" This question is a cry of despair coupled with fear of the future and the unknown. In time we can learn to say, "I don't know what I can do at this moment, but I know I can handle this. Thank God I don't have to face this issue by myself. I can learn and become a different person."

We limit our growth and recovery by our beliefs and thoughts. For many, the greatest prison is the locked door of their minds. We become and act out the rehearsed script in our minds.

Many years ago in a small town in the British Isles, a new jail was constructed that claimed to have an escape-proof cell. Harry Houdini, the great escape artist known all over the world, was invited to come and test it to see if it really was escape-proof. He accepted the invitation, having once boasted that no jail could hold him.

Houdini entered the cell, and the jailer closed the door behind him. Houdini listened to the sound of the key being slipped into the lock. The jailer withdrew the key and left. Houdini took out his tools and started the process of working on that cell door. But it didn't work out the way he expected. Nothing seemed to work, and the hours passed. He was puzzled because he'd never failed to open a locked door.

Finally the great Houdini admitted defeat. But when he leaned against the door in resigned exhaustion, it suddenly opened. The jailer had never locked it. The only place the door was locked was—as you can guess—in Houdini's mind.

I've done it and so have you; we've locked ourselves in because of what we've thought and believed. As a result we lock ourselves away from being able to change. Instead of enjoying the assurance and freedom that come from belonging to God, we become the negative people we imagine ourselves to be.

Nathaniel Hawthorne captured the dilemma beautifully in *The House of Seven Gables*: "What other dungeon is so dark as one's own heart! What jailer so inexorable as one's self!"

If you are on the verge of giving up, you're probably familiar with the phrase "I'm ready to throw in the towel!" Perhaps you've felt like saying it at one time or another in your life. You could even be saying it now because you don't feel as though you have any more to give. As one man said, "There's nothing left for me to do. I feel empty. I don't have any hope left."

John Karetji, a pastor from Indonesia, says he made that statement during a difficult time in his life. A man came to him and asked if he knew where the phrase about throwing in the towel came from. He replied that he didn't. The man went on to tell him that it's a phrase used in boxing. When the manager standing outside the ring sees that his fighter can't make it any longer in the boxing match, he throws the towel into the ring, signifying that they are giving up.

Did you notice? It's not the boxer who has the towel, it's the manager. It's not the boxer who can throw in the towel, only the manager. Only the one who sent the boxer into the ring can throw in the towel.

We may feel like the boxer who wants to call it quits. But we were sent into the ring of life by someone else. *Remember who it was who sent you into the ring!* Jesus said, "I will never leave you nor forsake you," and, "Lo, I am with you always."

Survivors Don't Become Bitter

Survivors *don't allow themselves to be bitter.* They refuse to live in the past or permit a situation to stop them in their tracks with no hope for the future. Bitterness comes from focusing on the unfairness of whatever has happened. It's like a warplane's radar locking onto a target. Bitterness leads to resentment, and the bitter person becomes the victim.

Many of the people I've seen who were stuck in their grief were there because of feelings of resentment. They built a dam around their bitterness instead of allowing it to drain away. Their resentment may have been against God, against the doctors, against the driver of the car that hit their son and left him in a coma, against the child who was into drugs and disruptive or against themselves. In each case they injured themselves and hindered their own growth more than anyone else's.

A man named Martin found this to be true while battling inoperable cancer. Here is his story:

I am free, free, free! Free in spirit, free in mind, free in expression. Nothing in the outer world can bind me or limit me. I am free from care, free to be happy, free to be loving and sharing today, free to be what God created me to be....

Jesus has shown me the why of suffering. I've found out that the person who must endure suffering will benefit from it if he is attentive to what the Lord is saying to him. As I look back over my life, I can personally testify that I could easily have done without many joyful experiences, but I could not have spared one valuable spiritual lesson I have learned from sorrow! Why? Because "God whispers in our pleasures but shouts in our pain"! The Lord forces us by our distresses to pay attention to His voice.

While such times of testing are not pleasant to endure, we must wait patiently for Him to accomplish His wise purposes. If we avoid becoming bitter in our earthly trials, we will learn the lessons of grace which only adversity can bring to the teachable heart. Those who accept troubles graciously grow rich by their losses, rise by their falls, and find new life in Christ by dying to self.

Often when God brings pressure into our lives, His purpose is to give us more power.[6]

Sometimes in discussing a painful situation, you hear someone say, "Don't tell me to forgive them! I'm not about to, and they don't deserve it!"

The natural response of anger and resentment causes pain, to be sure. And too often we choose to let it stay in our lives and gain a foothold. If your crisis involves another person, you may want to write a letter (don't mail it!) to either the event itself or the person involved. Write as much as you can each time under the headings "I resent ... " and "I wish ... " In time, your bitterness will lift, and that's the first step toward forgiveness.

A similar problem that will keep a person and the entire family stuck in the past is an attitude of resignation: "I give up. Why try? Nothing will change. This will always be the problem." You believe you're defeated already, so you don't give God much room to work in the crisis or in your heart. There were times when I wondered about our daughter, "How long will this go on? It's been three years already!"

Sometimes resignation is reflected in martyrdom. Martyrs complain and sulk, have low-grade depression or complain to just about anyone they meet about their difficulties. Unfortunately, in time this attitude will push others away.

Survivors Want to Learn and Grow

Survivors are those *who want to learn and grow.* They are overcomers.

In the Book of Revelation, we find statements to the churches that are being judged. Each time there are words of great hope and encouragement given to "him who overcomes." It is to the overcomers that the Lord makes these promises (emphasis added):

To him who *overcomes,* I will grant to eat from the tree of life, which is in the Paradise of God (2:7).

He who *overcomes* shall not be hurt by the second death (2:11).

To him who *overcomes* I will give some of the hidden manna, and I will give him a white stone, and a new name written on the stone which no one knows but he who receives it (2:17).

And he who *overcomes,* and he who keeps My deeds until the end, to him I will give authority over the nations ... and I will give him the morning star (2:26-28).

He who *overcomes* shall thus be clothed in white garments; and I will not erase his name from the book of life, and I will confess his name before my Father, and before His angels (3:5).

He who *overcomes,* I will make him a pillar in the temple of My God, and he will not go out from it anymore; and I will write upon him the name of My God, and the name of the city of My God, the New Jerusalem, which comes down out of heaven from My God, and My new name (3:12).

He who *overcomes,* I will grant to him to sit with Me on My throne, as I also overcame and sat down with My Father on His throne (3:21).

Tom Sullivan has been a frequent guest on the "Good Morning America" program. He also did some guest appearances on "M*A*S*H" and "Fame" and had a part in *Airport '77*. Tom holds two National Championship records in wrestling and was on the 1958 Olympic team for our country. He holds a degree from Harvard in clinical psychology; he is a musician and author, he runs six miles a day on the beach, he sky dives ... and he is blind. That's right, Tom is blind. He can't see a thing. His life was portrayed in the gripping film *If You Could See What I Hear.*

When he speaks to large crowds, the audience is with him all the way, listening, applauding, laughing and learning from a man who cannot see the enjoyment on their faces.

In his presentation, he has one major point: "You've got a disadvantage? Take advantage of it! People don't buy similarity. They buy differences." A disadvantage is what makes you stand out. Think about it. If you're similar to everyone else, you blend in and you're lost in the crowd.

Tom shared about the first time he realized he was blind. He was eight years old. He was in his backyard and he heard some new sounds—the crack of a bat as it hit a ball and the thud of the ball as it struck the glove.

He listened some more and decided they were playing a game. Did he get discouraged because he was blind and couldn't see what was happening? Not at all. He found a rock and a stick and taught himself how to bat. He wasn't sure where to hit, so he devised a target to aim at. He set up a transistor radio on a tree stump, walked back a few steps and began to practice. He practiced so much that eventually he could hit the radio every time.

After a while he told his dad that he wanted to play baseball. Imagine his father's reaction: "You want to do *what?*" Well, actually his dad said, "Really?... uh, which position?" Tom said, "I want to be a pitcher." Can you imagine the silence that hung in the air after that statement? His dad talked to the manager of the local Little League team and was able to get Tom on the team. And he pitched. They had another boy stand next to him to catch the ball when the catcher threw it back.

In Tom's presentation he says to the audience, "Can you picture this little frightened nine-year-old boy coming up to the plate, knowing that a blind kid is on the mound ready to throw a ball at him?" After he knocked out several boys, he switched to wrestling. Probably a collective sigh of relief went up from every Little League team.

Tom has a great sense of humor and the ability to pop out his glass eyes; he claims he won a few wrestling matches that way.[7]

It's an amazing story. Tom had a choice between cynical self-pity or learning to live a courageous life. Each of us has the same choice. Listen to one last statement by this courageous man.

"I've determined that my disadvantage in life is blindness," Tom Sullivan says. "I will therefore become, as a blind person, all that I can possibly be. That will become my distinctive message."[8]

Survivors Live in the Present and Look to the Future

A characteristic of those who cope is that they *live in the present* and *have a future perspective*. They seek to learn from what has happened to them and not live with regrets. They also learn to view the future as an opportunity, not a threat.

Most of the opportunities that will arise in the future are completely unknown to us. As Dr. Lloyd Ogilive says,

The sure sign that we have an authentic relationship with God is that we believe more in the future than in the past. God graciously divided our life into days and years so that we could let go of yesterdays and anticipate our tomorrow. For our tomorrow, He gives us the gift of expectation and excitement.[9]

Survivors Find Comfort in the Scriptures

Holding on to *the truth of Scripture* and its promises will help individuals and families survive. God said, "Be strong and courageous! Do not tremble or be dismayed, for the LORD your God is with you wherever you go" (Jos 1:9). He also promised, "For I know the plans that I have for you ... plans for welfare and not for calamity to give you a future and a hope" (Jer 29:11,).

It's vital to look to the future, even with its unknowns, for that is what can guide what we do now. Dr. Paul Walker tells of his experience with a survivor who focused on the future.

Do not worry about your life, what you will eat or drink; or about your body, what you will wear. Is not life more important than food, and the body more important than clothes? Look at the birds of the air; they do not sow or reap or store away into barns and yet your heavenly Father feeds them. Are you not more valuable than they? Who of you by worrying can add a single hour to his life? (Mt 6:25-27, NIV)

The key here is sanctification. The word sanctity means "to set apart and make holy." It is to consecrate and prepare for service. What this passage says is that as we sanctify our tomorrow we deal with the precious present. All we have is the now, and this now is to be lived out according to the highest priorities given to us by God in the fulfillment of the self. We are to allow tomorrow to take care of itself or, in other words, to commit the future into the hands of a loving God.

This idea of sanctifying tomorrow was brought to me by a man who was dying with cancer. Throughout the whole ordeal of his sickness, he seemed to maintain a sense of enthusiasm and strength that was astounding. Time and time again he came near death, but each time he would rally, to the amazement of doctors, nurses, family, and friends.

On one occasion I was called to the hospital because death was imminent. When I arrived, he was in a coma, and we all thought it was the end. But once again he endured and was able to return home.

During this period, I asked him, "How are you able to survive these close bouts with death? What is your secret?" In answer he said:

When it became certain that I had an inoperable cancer, I made a deal with the Lord.

First, I promised to live every moment of my life like it was the only moment I would have.

Second, I sanctified all my tomorrows and put them in the Lord's hands for whatever He had planned.

Third, I pray every day for a miracle of healing but know that I've got a good deal either way. If I receive a miracle, it will be a tremendous testimony to the world of God's great power and grace. If I die, I will go home to be with the Lord, and in reality that will be an even better deal.

Whether I live or die, I can't lose![10]

In one of his books, Chuck Swindoll shared this insight:

How does the widow or widower go on after the flowers wilt and the grass begins to grow over the grave? How does the athlete go on after age or injury takes its toll and someone younger takes his or her place? How does the mother go on after the children grow up and no longer need her? How does the victim move beyond the abuse or injustice without turning bitter?

How does the patient go on after the physician breaks the news about the dreaded biopsy? How does the divorcée go on after the divorce is final? How does anyone press on when the bottom drops out? What's the secret?

Well, I'm not sure I would call it a secret, but I have recently discovered some principles from Scripture that have certainly come to my rescue. They emerge from the life of David when he found himself unable to escape tough times.

It happened when David and his fellow warriors were returning from battle. Exhausted, dirty, and anxious to get home, they came upon a scene that took their breath away. What was once their own quiet village was now smoldering ruins; and their wives and children had been kidnapped by the same enemy forces that had burned their homes to the ground. Their initial reactions?

"So David and his men wept aloud until they had no strength left to weep" (1 Sm 30:4, NIV).

As if that were not bad enough, David's own men turned against him, and talk of mutiny swirled among the soldiers.

"David was greatly distressed because the men were talking of stoning him; each one was bitter in spirit because of his sons and his daughters" (30:6).

Those descriptive words, "greatly distressed," represent deep anguish and intense depression. If ever a man felt like hanging it up, David must have at that moment. But he didn't.

What did he do instead? Read this very carefully: "But David found strength in the Lord his God" (30:6).

He got alone and "gave himself a good talking to," as my mother used to say. He poured out his heart before the Lord ... got things squared away vertically, which helped clear away the fog horizontally. He did not surrender to hard times. Why not? How did he go on? By refusing to focus on the present situation only.

What happens when we stay riveted to the present misery? One of two things: either we blame someone (which can easily make us bitter) or we submerge in self-pity (which paralyzes us). Going on with our lives will never occur as long as we concentrate all our attention on our present pain.[11]

Instead of retaliating or curling up in a corner to lick his wounds, David called to mind that this event was no mistake. The Lord wasn't absent. On the contrary, He was in full control. Bruised and bloody, David faced the test head-on and refused to throw in the towel. Perhaps you've already noticed that throughout these characteristics, we keep going back again and again to the Word of God. It really is our ultimate survival guide. Your faith in God and His Son Jesus and your commitment to follow the Scriptures will be your source of strength that will not crumble.

Survivors Learn to Resolve Conflicts

One of the steps that helps families survive is learning to manage and resolve their conflicts. Families that don't do this heap one conflict upon another. When a new conflict occurs, they respond to it out of the contamination of all the unresolved issues in their reservoir. If you haven't learned to resolve conflicts before a crisis, you're not likely to do it during one.

When family members know conflicts aren't resolved, some may take the attitude, "Why even bother?" and not listen to or engage others in conversation. A healthy family overrides its fears and discovers ways to make things different. Members learn to solve problems and are willing to listen to one another and try something new. This approach is a source of encouragement and hope in the midst of heartache.

It's also important to determine which problems are worth tackling, which are not and which ones can be resolved. At times, you'll need to postpone problem solving or take time out.

Successful families believe that each person has the ability to handle the adversity. They don't suffocate one another with words like "You should ... " or "You ought to ... " or by being overbearing with advice. Rather, they encourage one another. Unconditional love is the backbone for their relationships.

Successful families also respect their members' personality differences. If a person needs to talk or do something—or needs privacy and quiet—that's all right.

Survivors Enjoy Life

Those who survive crisis have an established pattern of *enjoying life*. They can laugh even during the difficult times. It's a way of taking a break from the heaviness of the crisis.

The first time I experienced this was as a youth pastor when I led a group of twenty-five high schoolers on a camping trip into the high Sierra Mountain Range in southern California. One morning two of the boys set out on their own to climb the face of a sheer rock protruding hundreds of feet into the sky. One of the boys fell four hundred feet to his death. For hours a sense of heavy gloom lay on all of us. After dinner the campers began cracking jokes and were laughing and joking for over an hour. Other adults wondered, "How could they?" But those kids needed to take that break. We all do at times.

A wife shared her story about the value of humor:

We try to treat things seriously that need it and poke fun at the rest. We often ask ourselves, "Will this be funny later?" and lots of petty irritants are. I'll give you an example. We headed out for a company potluck dinner one evening in a bit of a fluster because we were about five minutes late and my husband was supposed to give the invocation. At the car trunk, juggling keys and a casserole, he spilled the hot casserole on his hand and down his trousers. He flipped it onto the lawn (killing the grass, by the way) and raced back inside to change clothes. We raced off and were halfway there when a police officer pulled us over. We had missed a new "No left turn" sign at an intersection. Of course the officer wanted to see my husband's license and you know where his wallet was? Right! At home in the other trousers. There we sat explaining spilled casseroles and changed clothes to the officer. She let us go with a warning. No one would have made up a story like ours. We arrived at the dinner and my husband said, "I'm sorry we're late, but I am very thankful just to be here. Let me tell you why ..." His humor changed a blood-pressure-raising series of incidents into a good story.

One final example comes from our friend Sally, a courageous woman who was born with a rare degenerative disease that slowly constricts her body. She spends her time in a wheelchair and was in danger of dying when we talked with her. Her spine had bent so much that she was down to 30 percent of her normal breathing capacity. She was slowly suffocating.

A major operation was her only hope; her back would be cut open from top to bottom and stainless steel inserts put into each vertebra to help straighten her spine. "Normal" life in which one walks and runs would never be possible, but life itself would be possible.

As we talked she joked about being a "bionic woman" and predicted she'd need a whole new wardrobe. We asked why new clothes and she said, "Because I'll be six-foot-seven with all those metal spacers in me. And think what havoc I'll cause in airport metal detectors!"

"Seriously, Sally," we said, "how can you laugh so much about this?"

"You know what they say," she replied. "It's either laugh or cry."

And laughter often is the balm we need for the silliness, madness and ironies of daily life.[12]

Survivors Adapt to Change

Survivors are *flexible, resilient and adaptable.* The lack of these qualities makes a huge difference in the way a person copes with life. In other words, the more rigid a person is, the less hopeful his life is, because rigidity makes changing direction difficult. Perfectionists, and those who must have everything under control, have a hard time handling crises. How do you think others would describe you? Do you think they would say you are rigid or flexible? Ask your spouse or a trusted friend if you're unsure of the answer.

Sometimes we think of survivors as being extraordinary individuals. A few are, but most are not. Survivors—people of hope and faith—have their faults and flaws. They are like anyone else, with one exception. They have a different way of thinking about some things. Here's a reminder of some of the attitudes that characterize survivors.

1. Survivors say, "I will examine the future and let it guide what I do in the present." Many people, upon reaching middle age or old age, move into despair. They have regrets over the way they have lived and they realize there's little time left to change things. Perhaps by examining our priorities and values at a younger age we can gain better direction for our lives and be satisfied in later years.

According to the Scriptures, living life with a forward view is healthy and hopeful. Jesus said: "Most assuredly, I say to you, he who believes in Me, the works that I do he will do also; and greater works than these he will do, because I go to My Father. And whatever you ask in My name, that I will do, that the Father may be glorified in the Son. If you ask anything in My name, I will do it" (Jn 14:12-14, NKJV).

God asked Abraham to look into the future. In Genesis 13:14-16 He instructed Abraham to gaze northward, southward, eastward and westward at the land He was giving to him. Then in verse 17 God told Abraham, then called Abram, to do something very strange: "Arise, walk about the land through its length and breadth; for I will give it to you."

Dr. Lloyd Ogilvie comments:

In order to build in Abram the confidence of a risk taker, the Lord had to help him claim the reality of the seemingly impossible. He not only gave him a vision, but he also made him walk through that vision until he made it really his own.

God does the same thing with you and me. First he gives us the impossible dream, then he helps us envision what it will be like to possess our possession, and then through our imagination he helps us persistently imagine the reality. What is the dream for you?

Have you examined your future? Will you today?

2. *The survivor says, "No matter what happens, I will not allow myself to be defeated. I will keep on trying and will not give up."* Perseverance is a mark of hope and faith. It is essential to realizing God's blessing. Do you persevere and keep on trying?

3. *The survivor says, "I am a fortunate person, regardless of what I have experienced."* You may be ignoring the blessings around you by focusing on your losses instead of your gains. There is always hope and the possibility of growth. You could be much worse off than you are. Survivors consistently take inventory of what they have rather than what they do not have. When was the last time you took such an inventory?

4. *The survivor says, "I will take advantage of every available opportunity."* I have spoken with handicapped people who look for every opportunity to create and grow. Perhaps the more handicapped someone is, the more he appreciates what he can experience. We all need to look at life through thankful

eyes and seize the opportunities around us. What opportunities are around you right now that you could take advantage of and use to generate even more hope for yourself?

5. *The survivor says, "I can accept my imperfections and learn to enjoy life and give to others."* Survivors don't strive for perfection; they realize it's impossible to be perfect. But they do work toward excellence. What are your imperfections? Do you dwell on these deficits, or do you direct your energy toward improving what can be improved while accepting what can't be changed?

6. *Survivors say, "I can find meaning in situations and events that involve suffering or great loss."* Where meaninglessness exists, there is no hope. Sometimes the meaning of a negative or hurtful event cannot be seen until much later. Over a period of twenty-two years my wife and I learned this lesson and this attitude through the life and death of our son, Matthew.

You must grieve your losses and then come to the point of replacing the "why" questions with the "how" questions: "How can I learn through this experience? How can I grow through this? How can God be glorified through this experience?"

7. *Survivors say, "I will not allow myself to behave as a victim."* Even in the midst of the hurt and pain of life, survivors learn to move on and they choose not to see themselves as helpless victims. For most people, this involves a change in thinking. Do you see yourself as a victim? If so, does this attitude create more victim experiences for you?

8. *Survivors say, "I'm determined to keep pushing ahead."* Survivors are able to make and keep commitments. They are able to build their lives on Jeremiah 29:11 and 33:3 and allow God to guide them: "For I know the thoughts that I think toward you, says the Lord, thoughts of peace and not of evil, to give you a future and a hope" (NKJV); "Call to Me, and I will answer you, and show you great and mighty things, which you do not know" (NKVJ). In what ways are you living in the past? In what ways are you determinedly moving ahead in life?

9. Survivors say, "I am willing to grow and change and learn new roles." I often see this attitude in divorced persons as they learn to function as both mom and dad to their children. I see this in men who are able to learn to be affectionate, demonstrative and feeling-oriented in relationships. Every one of us has an opportunity to grow. If we don't, our only option is stagnation. In what ways are you growing and changing? In what ways do you need to expand in order to help yourself and those around you?

10. Survivors say, "I want to be involved with people who will build me up and help me grow." We were never meant to make it alone. But it's foolish to surround ourselves with people who fill our mind with negative talk and example. We can't grow and be blessed if you spend all your time with sick people.

Healthy people don't tear you down or drain you. You need people in your life to give you strength. You need encouragers. Who are the significant people in your life, and in what ways do they help you mature and grow stronger? Who do you pray for? Who prays for you?

11. Survivors say, "I can face the challenges of life and handle the stresses and crises of life without denying their existence or giving up." I especially like this last attitude of a survivor. It's not just what happens to us; it's how we respond to what happens to us that's so important. It's the ability to take James 1:2-3 and apply it to our lives. Remember, a survivor is a person who makes sense out of what happens to him. Never, never let your hand slip off of your hope.[13]

In the first chapter I shared about a friend of mine afflicted by multiple sclerosis. Dave is surviving. During the beginning years of his disease he experienced the pain of divorce as well. In 1990, when he was still somewhat ambulatory, he remarried a woman fourteen years younger. In preparation for their life together with a disease that would become progressively worse, they both attended several national conferences on multiple sclerosis to learn as much as they could about what to expect in the future. Lisa began cooking his specialized diet even before their marriage. They discussed issues they thought they would face in the future, including the age factor, who would eventually support the family, whether or not to have children.

At the time of writing this book they have two children and Dave is at home. He had to retire on disability insurance from his work. Lisa teaches school until noon and then returns home. I asked Dave, "How have you made it? How do you go on?" This is what he told me:

First of all, it is my relationship with the Lord. My faith in Him has sustained me. Then it's been Lisa. In our wedding vows she pledged to be my hands and feet. And more and more she's doing this. I've learned to make adjustments in my life for what I could no longer do. It was difficult to respond to letters and E-Mail with my computer. So I was able to obtain a voice activated computer and I'm able to be as verbal as ever in my responses.

Another factor has been the memorizing of God's Word. I recite the verses out loud, which strengthens my mouth muscles. With MS, your speech tends to get sloppy, and doing this helps to keep this from occurring. You lose so many abilities as it is with MS. Each time you lose one you have to fight the tendency to give up on everything. When each ability goes you have to grieve over that loss just like you did before. You never finish the process of grieving throughout this. But memorizing God's Word gives you the inner strength and confidence as well as depending upon the Lord.

Do you see all the factors involved in this man's survival? His faith in God and his reliance upon others, especially his wife, were strong factors. Dave wouldn't give up. He moved ahead with his life with a new family, making adjustments and discovering new ways to function, relying upon God's Word and facing his losses by grieving over them. This is what it takes to move on in life.

I urge you to pray this prayer by Chuck Swindoll,

It's not often, Father, that we make such a statement, but today we thank You for the injustices that have crippled us and broken us and crushed us.

We want to express our appreciation for the things that have brought us to the place of submission. The only way we can look is up.

We express our gratitude for the things You have taught us through blindness and loss and paralysis; for growth through broken dreams, dissolved partnerships, illness, and sadness; for the character development through insecurity, failure, and even divorce. We see the storm, but we are beginning to see You beyond the storm. How essential is our attitude!

Thank you especially for helping us conquer our cynicism.

I pray for those in these and a hundred other categories, that we may be able to go beyond them and find in Jesus Christ the strength to go on, especially for those who, only a few moments ago, had just about decided to give up. I pray that they will rather give it all to You in full surrender.

In the strong name of Jesus Christ, the Conqueror, I pray. Amen.[14]

Hope Makes a Difference

Hope looks for the good in people instead of harping on the worst in them.

Hope opens doors where despair closes them.

Hope discovers what can be done instead of grumbling about what cannot be done.

Hope draws its power from a deep trust in God and the basic goodness of mankind.

Hope "lights a candle" instead of "cursing the darkness."

Hope regards problems, small or large, as opportunities.

Hope cherishes no illusions, nor does it yield to cynicism.

—Source Unknown

ELEVEN

— ◆ —

Adopting a Plan for Resilience

How old are you? I mean your exact age. It's all right, you can say it. No one else will hear. Not even me. Your age is important. You need to look at it to determine which of life's transitions you've already experienced and which ones are yet to occur. Perhaps you've never given them any thought. You're not alone.

Do you know what a life transition is? It's a bridge between two different stages of life. Any new change carries elements of risk, insecurity and vulnerability. You move from a time of certainty to a time of uncertainty back to certainty.

Even the normal passages we go through in the journey of adulthood can lead to a crisis. They can include such events as getting married, having a child, the child becoming an adolescent, a vocational change, hitting the empty nest, caring for aging parents, identity change, mid-life transitions, retirement and even specific birthdays such as forty, fifty and sixty-five.

Some people have never adjusted to the normal changes and transitions of life, which keeps them from anticipating the future. That's too bad. Some who marry spend so much time working on the marriage that they fail to spend time preparing to become parents. And when the child arrives they aren't ready for the demands of the newborn nor the impact on "the couple relationship." Now the focus is on trying to learn to be parents, and the marriage is neglected. In a few years when the divorce occurs, which was avoidable, the couple wonders what happened.

We don't often anticipate transitions once we become adults. In fact, some people just move from one stage of adulthood to another without giving the future a second thought. That's too bad, because they often end up wondering how they got into the situation they're in. They don't prepare for change—good, bad or indifferent. When we fail to handle the changes in our lives, they can become crises.

For some couples the empty nest is a major crisis. Their sense of loss and change is very real. They feel a mingling of numerous emotions as expressed in Ecclesiastes 3:1-8—a time of weeping, laughing, mourning, healing, loving, releasing, losing and embracing. The atmosphere of the home changes. There are fewer choices to make, less confusion and noise. Old patterns of shopping, cooking, scheduling—use of time—will change. New roles will have to be established and new pressures may occur.

Needs formerly filled by children will be diverted to someone else for fulfillment. These needs include communication, affection and companionship. If a couple rushes toward each other, demanding that their partner replace previous interaction they had with their child, they may instead push each other away.

Frequently the upheaval of children preparing to leave home hits at the same time as the mid-life transition. What do parents say to themselves as children leave? Listen to their thoughts.

"I miss the early years with my children. I was so tied up in work at that time."

"The nest doesn't seem to empty as fast as I want. They're sure slow in moving out."

"I looked at that small chair and started to cry. It seemed like yesterday that my son was sitting in it."

"I'm sure I'll be glad when they will leave. But won't I feel useless?"

"That room seemed so empty when he left."

"I'm looking forward to a new job! This time for pay!"

"Now that they're gone, we sit, we don't talk, don't look at each other. Nothing!"

"Parenting is hard work and I want to get out of this job."

"We married at twenty and had the first one at twenty-two. The last one came at thirty-four. He left when he turned twenty-four. Why didn't someone tell us it would take twenty-nine years until we were alone again as a couple!"

"We're adjusted to them being gone. I hope none of them divorce or lose a job and have to move back. I like this setup!"

"I don't want to build my happiness on when they call, write or visit. I need my own life now."

"They left too soon, married too young and had kids too soon. I hope they realize I'm not their baby-sitter. I raised one family but I'm not going to raise another."

"I've done what I could. They're in the Lord's hands now. And I guess they always have been, come to think of it."

Preparing for Change

One of the best ways to prepare for your future is to first deal with your past. When you're still trying to please a parent, or your life is damaged because of abuse, rejection, abandonment or neglect, your energy for handling the present and future is limited. It's like trying to progress through life with an anchor tied around one leg. You end up with an overabundance of baggage, which interferes with your mobility.

Years ago I wrote a book titled *Making Peace with Your Past.* The theme was that we are able to handle our future in a healthier way when we have resolved what can be resolved from our past. This means that we honestly face what has occurred in the past, we talk about it to those who were involved and we take steps to correct the aftereffects.

Sometimes this means that we have to learn to respond differently to those in the past and the present. It often means substituting forgiveness for retribution. But it also involves identifying and using all of the positives from our past as well.

With any crisis experience we can choose to become a "yesterday person" or a "tomorrow person." Sometimes people in our past have damaged or hurt us and contributed to our difficulties. As Jack Hayford, a well-known pastor, describes it:

> Predecessors, plain people such as our parents, teachers or friends (even those disposed to our best interest) can cast shadows over our tomorrows. They may have set boundaries on our lives, limiting our view of ourselves or our potential. Or they may have been confined by boundaries of their own which found exact or mirrored images in us. But in either case, our predecessors often shape us, leaving an imprint which may be the source of our own present frustration.
>
> How can we deal with this?
>
> First, though God wants to free us unto tomorrow, He won't allow us to blame yesterday. Neither will He allow us to cast blame on anything or anybody who seems to restrict our tomorrows.[1]

The next step in preparing for your future is to take action *now* for future events. Dr. Gary Collins refers to Alvin Toffler's book *Future Shock,* especially as it relates to the family.

> When Alvin Toffler wrote about handling change, he seemed to suggest two broad strategies for coping. We can reduce the amount of novelty and innovation that comes into our lives, and we can increase our abilities to cope and adapt. Some of Toffler's suggestions for accomplishing this, and his "strategies for survival" in a world of rapid change, may not have been practical. But he proclaimed that we don't have to mope about, wringing our hands in despair, standing like helpless victims of change without hope or determination to resist. Instead, we can take action to move toward family goals in the present, knowing that this will determine, in large part, how we cope with continual change, anticipate family shocks, prepare for the unexpected, and move confidently into the future.[2]

When you consider your life for the next ten years and begin to anticipate the possible changes or transitions and how they may affect you, you will be better prepared. You're less likely to be surprised or thrown off course.

When I was a youth pastor in the early sixties, there were three hundred teenagers in our church. Time after time parents would come into the office visibly upset, saying, "I don't know what's going on with this kid. It seems like just yesterday she was a child. Now that the teen years have hit, I don't understand her."

I thought then, "Why didn't you prepare yourself in advance for this stage? It's possible to do so."

Perhaps that's why I've always tried to anticipate what the next few years could bring in my life. You can do it too.

During any major transition, people must restructure how they view their role in life and plan how to incorporate the change. Most people wait until they're in the midst of the transition before thinking about it. Most of us need to put forth tremendous effort to give up old patterns of thinking and activity and develop new ones. Whether or not this transition becomes disastrous depends upon a person's ability to handle this process of change in a healthy way. This means planning in advance and learning to live a life of hope and faith.

One of the greatest determinants of whether a transition involves excessive stress and crisis potential is the timing of such an event. Serious difficulties can occur when the accomplishment of tasks associated with a particular stage of development is disrupted or made extremely difficult. For example, if you wait for fifteen years of marriage to have your first child, the intrusion of a demanding third party may be difficult. If your teenager suddenly becomes a paraplegic because of a diving accident, you and your teen must rethink your whole lives.

We do not have to be victims of the future. We can decide now how we will respond to future transitions.

I live in southern California, the earthquake capital of the nation. When you look at a map indicating all of the earthquake faults, it's difficult to count them. We know we will have earthquakes. We expect them.

Several years ago I was in the Whittier quake just seven miles from the epicenter. At first I heard a roar like a freight train. At the time I was playing in a racquetball court and my initial thought was that the aerobics class upstairs was especially loud that morning. Then it dawned on me—there was no aerobics class upstairs! Just then the walls began to sway and the lights went out. We were out of that building in seconds! The building wasn't damaged, partly because of the way it was constructed. Like many of the newer buildings here, it was constructed with flexibility to sway back and forth several feet. It was designed to handle future tremors.

We, too, can prepare for many of life's future tremors. We live at a time in which we are not lacking for information or assistance to help us prepare for the future. All we need to do is confront it and apply it.

Gary Smalley shares the story of one of his childhood experiences:

When I was about twelve years old, I got the scare of my life. It was the worst thing that ever happened to me. In fact, I'm amazed that I'm alive today to tell this story.

My family was living in the state of Washington, out in the country. One fall day I was outside playing with my best friend. Having great fun, we weren't paying much attention to the clock. As the sun crept toward the horizon, we suddenly realized it was time to be heading home. So, like the two adventurous boys we were, we decided to take a shortcut through a wooded area.

We had no path to follow, but that didn't bother us. We were just running along, the wind whistling past our ears. And then, all of a sudden, we heard this deafening and horrifying rattling sound very close by. We stopped, froze, and listened. The sound was all around us, and it seemed to be coming from everywhere at once.

We looked at the ground. It was moving. We were in the middle of a field of rattlesnakes! Hundreds of them, in all sizes. And they were striking out blindly in all directions.

My friend and I knew we didn't have long to live.

Fortunately, we had the presence of mind to jump up on a snake-free log that was well above the ground. We yelled for help at the top of our lungs, but we were too deep into the woods for anyone to hear.

"What are we going to do?" my friend shouted.

"I don't know," I answered, "but we've got to do something soon because it's getting dark!" *Will the snakes crawl up onto our log?* I wondered.

Then one of us got the idea of breaking long branches off the log and using them as extended arms or "swords" to flip the writhing, rattling creatures out of our way as we cleared a path to make our escape. And that's what we did. One snake at a time—what seemed like one inch at a time—crying all the way, we made a path to the edge of that sea of snakes. The slightest slip or fall would have landed us on top of a half-dozen of them, but we kept moving.

We only had about thirty feet to cover to get into the clear, but it seemed to take forever. When we finally left the last snake behind, we were trembling and exhausted. But we gathered our remaining strength and ran home as fast as we could to report our own near-death experience.[3]

Gary goes on to describe how that day would have been different had they anticipated what they would encounter and prepared for it. If they had worn thick leather hip boots, not only could they have walked through the snake infested woods but their attitude would have been totally different. It's the same with us. When we prepare for the upsets of life, we handle them better.

An example of how to prepare for one future life transition is premarital counseling. Marriages *can* last. Divorce *is* avoidable. Information abounds on what makes a marriage work and last. But once again we must make the choice to discover the information and then apply it. (See my book *Secrets of a Lasting Marriage*, Regal Books.)

Stephen Covey, a motivational leader and author, talks about people who are either "reactive" or "proactive." Reactive people are strongly affected by their surroundings, whether it be events or people. They constantly build their emotional lives around the responses of others, which allows the weaknesses of others to dictate their own behavior. Even the weather can make or break their day. If the sun is shining, they feel good. But if dark clouds fill the sky, they feel gloomy.

Resilient (proactive) people, on the other hand, carry their own weather around with them. While the weather might alter their plans a bit, they have learned not to let it affect their basic attitude toward life.

Many of us are reactive when it comes to thinking about the crises and problems of the past. We continue to react to experiences from our past as though they are still happening. If we've never made that important transition of shedding the impact of the painful event, we end up feeling like a victim for the rest of our lives.

Proactive people can be just as aware of what is going on around them—whether it's related to the past or present—but they have learned to respond in a new way. As the adage goes, it's not *what happens to us* but *our response to what happens to us* that can help or hinder us.[4]

Even though our day-to-day experience can sometimes feel like drudgery, life is always full of twists and turns, bends in the road, U-turns, even temporary roadblocks and seeming dead ends. The journey uniquely blends acquiring and losing, receiving and giving away, holding and letting go.

Every transition carries with it seeds for growth, new insights, refinement and understanding. But in the midst of turmoil, sometimes the positive aspects seem too far in the future to be very real.

The best way to plan for change is to identify your expectations for life. Even if we don't stop to think about it, we all have timetables for our lives, don't we? In premarital counseling I ask couples when they expect to become parents, graduate from school, move to a higher level of responsibility in their careers, and so on. Some of them have developed very precise timetables. I find it interesting that many say they want to retire at fifty! Most people have their own expectations for when certain events will occur—a sort of mental clock that tells them whether they are on time or not in terms of the family life cycle. It's as though we believe we really have that much control over our lives.

Plan for Marriage

When couples marry, most assume they will stay married for life. They won't. At least 25 percent[5] won't. Many of these wouldn't end up as a statistic if they had prepared and planned in a realistic way for what a marriage relationship entails.

I see churches all over this country investing hours in couples to help them prepare for marriage. Some churches require thirty to fifty hours of preparation before the marriage and accountability involvement with an older mentor couple for the first three years of marriage. This is crisis prevention against divorce. And since 10 to 30 percent of couples dissolve their relationship before marrying, they too have avoided the crisis of divorce.

Couples need to know before marriage about the three peak danger times when couples divorce—at two years, seven years and fifteen years. They need to know before marriage the exact process or steps involved in falling out of love so they can take steps to ensure that doesn't happen. (See chapter 2 of *Secrets of a Lasting Marriage* for a complete presentation of this process.)

Plan for Parenthood and Possible Problems/Concerns

Couples need to plan to become parents before the child arrives. Some couples have actually spent hours interviewing other couples of preschoolers to discover what to expect, how to plan and what to avoid. This too is crisis prevention.

Even when a child goes through the transition of entering school, new issues come forward. The parents, through the child, are now on public display. Children don't edit what they say. Home life can be quite a revelation. There can also be conflict with school or a spouse's style of discipline, and great adjustments in the time schedule.

Plan for the Unexpected

When an event does not take place "on time," according to someone's individual expectations, a crisis may result. Many mothers face an adjustment when the youngest child leaves home. You can plan for this predictable stage of an empty nest. But when a child doesn't leave home at the expected time, a crisis can often occur for both parents and child.

Our daughter returned home not once, not twice, not three, but four times between the ages of twenty-one and twenty-six! Talk about a revolving door. Twice she brought home a cat, and when she moved out the cats didn't! What will you do if a child moves back home with his or her three children? What if your child divorces? How would you handle that?

When an event occurs too early, it can keep us from preparing adequately. A young mother who is widowed has to support her family during a time when most of her friends are married. An oldest son may suddenly have to quit college and take over the family business because of some unexpected event, even though he feels ill-equipped for this new role.

Today a revolution is taking place. There are dramatic changes in the family life cycle. If you use your parents as a model of what to expect, you may make some mistakes. Today, children leave childhood earlier. Puberty seems to arrive earlier. It's as though childhood is shortened and adolescence is lengthened as more young adults live at home for a longer period of time. Young adults take longer to grow up and assume adult responsibilities, and they live longer than previous generations.

Another change that can bring about a crisis condition is when stepparents or "late baby" couples struggle with their own adjustments to aging while also dealing with turbulent teenagers. Women want children but they're postponing pregnancy. Why not have a baby at forty-five? But how does a sixty-year-old parent handle a fifteen-year-old?

Middle age is a time of gathering and accumulating. As R. Scott Sullender describes it:

The middle years of adult life are spent building. We build a family, a career, a home and place in the community. It is a time for planting roots deep into the soil of our psyches. We build memories that last a lifetime. We form deep emotional attachments with one another. The latter half of life, however, is a time when what has been built up gradually dissolves. One by one (or, sometimes, all at once) we must let go of family, career and home.[6]

Prepare for Middle Age

Have you thought much about the middle years? Have you made any plans for them yet?

Some people have attributed to God a morbid sense of humor. Why? Because whenever a parent reaches his mid-life passage, he usually has a teen who is going through a similar adolescent transition! It is a case of the groping leading the groping. It is not just that one person in transition is in charge of another person in transition, like two people on different merry-go-rounds trying to keep in touch; rather, the two transitions act upon one another.

The youngster moving into adolescence becomes a reminder to the parent that he or she is moving into old age.[7]

I doubt if there is anyone left who hasn't heard about the male mid-life crisis. But there's still an abundance of misunderstanding and misinformation about it. What we do know for sure is that almost all men go through some type of mid-life *transition*. This is a normal process in which the person reevaluates purposes and values. Sometimes he makes changes, sometimes not. The classic mid-life crisis hits a minority of men with its predictable upheaval and radical change of life. But for the most part, this crisis is preventable. The prime candidates for mid-life crisis are men who have the sole source of their identity tied up in their work, who have no close male friendships and who don't share their feelings.

Middle age is no longer the late thirties and forties. It's been pushed into the fifties. It's been said that fifty is what forty used to be. Chronological age doesn't always match what people are experiencing internally. For many there seems to be a second adulthood in middle life. The average healthy man who reaches sixty-five can expect to live until eighty-one, while a cancer- and heart disease-free fifty-year-old woman will reach ninety-two![8] This is a big change from most of human history, when only one in ten people lived to be sixty-five.

Prepare for Physical Changes. Adulthood no longer begins at twenty-one and ends at sixty-five! Many transitions in life are related to the aging process, and they seem to accelerate in middle age. As we grow older, the dreams and beliefs of childhood begin to crumble and change.

Then come the physical losses attending the usual aging process. Ironically, one change typical of middle age involves gain—you know, those unwanted pounds and inches! We gradually lose our youth, our beauty, our smooth skin, our muscle tone, our shape, our hair, our vision and hearing, our sexual ability or interest and so on.

In the later years, the losses take on a different flavor. Now they seem to be more frequent, permanent and in many cases, negative. Who rejoices over losing hair and teeth or graduating to bifocals or even trifocals? We don't usually call these "growth experiences." Our losses now seem to build on other losses.[9]

In our younger years, we may have one or two physical problems, which are often correctable. But later on, body ailments accumulate faster than our ability to resolve them. Muscles don't work as well or recover as quickly. Our response time slows down.

Our eyeglasses prescription needs to be changed more often. One day we suddenly notice that people seem to be talking in softer tones. We soon have to turn up the television volume along with the thermostat!

The nature of the losses is compounded by their growing frequency. We don't usually lose many of our friends through death early in life. But in our later years, such loss becomes more frequent. The longer we live, the more friends and relatives we lose.

We seem to handle loss best when it is less frequent. But after mid-life, we typically move into a time zone of accumulated losses. It can be difficult to handle the next loss when we are still recovering from the present one. Our coping skills soon get overtaxed. If those skills were never highly developed to begin with, serious and frequent losses can hit us like a freight train.

Major changes create disequilibrium, and these changes seem to accelerate each year. There are people today who don't know how to be forty, fifty or sixty.

What do we do with the extra years? What do you do when there are no more opportunities for advancement in your company? When work opportunities shrink and longer life faces you, what do you do?

One of the most disruptive changes has been in careers. Traditionally, you worked at a job that was fairly secure until you were sixty-five. Then you retired and played. The upheaval of corporate life in America has generated individual and family crises. Companies have shrunk, changed direction or just disappeared. Information technology has replaced many blue-color jobs.

Prepare for Possible Job Loss or Change. You're no longer secure in your job when you are fifty years old. In fact, you may not have a job. For many, career divorce is just as painful as a marriage breakup.

Doctor Griff, a psychiatrist associated with Harvard, sees job loss as generating feelings similar to the humiliation found in the nightmare of being naked in a public place. Men used to think that when they were in their forties they should be preparing themselves for the next promotion. Now they think, "How do I prepare myself to start over if I'm dumped?"

In the early nineties alarms sounded for the fifty-five and older group. The Bureau of Labor Statistics showed that from October 1991 to October 1992 the unemployment rate for those who were fifty-five and older was seven times that of the age bracket sixteen to fifty-four.[10]

Peter Drucker has predicted that two-thirds of the managerial positions that existed in the late eighties will be gone by the year 2000.[11]

Jim Smoke, in the book *Facing Fifty*, writes:

The fifty-something people who had been looking forward to their fifties as a time of power, success and financial security suddenly found themselves filled with fear and worry as they scrambled to reshuffle their dreams. One fifty-something manager in a large worldwide company described this situation when he said, "When I finally got to the party, I found it was over ... and I had no place to go."[12]

This is not just a threat to our economic security but often to our identity as well.

Losing a job or a career can be immobilizing. And the onslaught of emotions it brings can debilitate you. Try dealing with fear, pain, blame, denial, anger, depression and no self-worth all at the same time. One of the biggest responses that comes and goes like an unwelcome guest is self-blame. You feel like a victim, stomped on and robbed by your profession. Many men today feel a sense of betrayal. When their job disappears they feel like asserting, "That isn't the way it was supposed to be!"

Job loss is disruptive to family life as well. For too long men have tended to have one source of self-identity—their work. For both men and women, having one identity source is a liability. Those who survive job loss and economic changes are those who have developed multiple identities.[13]

Survivors are those who don't let the future overwhelm them, but see it as a challenge that will involve multiple changes—a new lifestyle, new priorities, new standards and perhaps a new home. Some call this crisis the end of a life. Others call it a "redirection" or "exploring new opportunities."

Jim Smoke has some helpful suggestions for anyone going through a dramatic career change such as this. He says that survivors cut themselves loose emotionally from their old jobs. When they find a new job, it's important to commit to it in a new way. The old measures of success need to be abandoned. Status, security and salary must be substituted for your own new criteria.[14] This perspective can help you avoid a crisis in the future.

There is one group in our society who is experiencing their own unique crisis when it comes to the career arena—the Baby Boomers. They seem to have a high degree of discontent with their careers. The calm drive they expected is more like a giant roller coaster ride. Some have lost their jobs for all the typical reasons. Others selected the wrong job to begin with or purposely chose a career to counter their parents' expectations.

Baby Boomers have a higher level of dissatisfaction than the older generation. What they find in their job is less than they had hoped for. And because this generation is so committed to change and experimentation, they are less likely to have steady and predictable jobs during their middle and later years.

Prepare for Retirement and Old Age

Retirement used to be something you looked forward to at age sixty-five. For some it's a reward. For others it's a statement of your loss of value. This is one of the most difficult transitions of all. The younger the man or the higher his status, the more difficult it is to retire and the greater the fear of becoming just another retiree. Retirement includes many losses: loss of income, loss of status, loss of feeling significant, loss of being challenged by other good minds, loss of the source of who you are! For men especially retirement is a time of depression, and the suicide rate more than triples for men over sixty-five.

A teacher who realized he would have to retire in ten years determined to take charge of this transition. He began to take courses at the local college in subjects he thought he might have an interest in. He took up photography and began reading in areas he had never considered before. He also began developing a list of projects he would like to tackle, health and finances permitting, upon retirement. Since he would experience a significant loss in his life—his job and his livelihood—he planned in advance for a variety of replacements and worked through some of those feelings of loss.

He also had the foresight to develop hobbies he could enjoy whether his health was good or poor. By anticipating the future, he eliminated the possibility of the transition turning into a crisis.

This man actually developed a plan. Plan A consisted of making a list of all the desires he had for retirement, along with their possibilities, assuming good health and good finances, and that he and his spouse would be together or he would be alone. Plan B and Plan C allowed for certain variables in the plan.

Plan A	**Desires and Possibilities**
Good health	
Good finances	
Alone	
Together	

Plan B	**Desires and Possibilities**
Good health/poor finances	
Poor health/good finances	
Alone	
Together	

Plan C	**Desires and Possibilities**
Poor health	
Poor finances	
Alone	
Together	

When you think about, discuss and prepare for as many options as possible, you will feel more secure.

But there are other changes that occur at this stage of life. More and more retirees seek out the so-called comfort and support of a retirement community. Jim Smoke puts a different perspective on this option:

Retirement communities are filled with once-important people who are living out their lives in personal obscurity. While most probably enjoy their new life of leisure, many others turn to drugs and alcohol, the silent killers in scores of retirement enclaves across America, to deaden the pain caused by loss of identity and self-worth. Prescription drugs follow close behind as the killer of past dreams and present realities. As a result, in many instances retirement kills people quicker than most diseases. It happens because it takes something from them that many are not ready to give up: their identity. Mundane card games and craft classes after a daily round of golf cannot give meaning and purpose to life after he has impacted others' lives for 40 years.

In most cases, retired men lose their identities quicker and more often than retired women, perhaps because many women consider themselves still "employed" as homemakers, wives, and mothers. There are abundant tales of retired husbands following their wives around all day long, looking for some form of meaning and fulfillment.[15]

There definitely is a crisis for many in older age. Some people suddenly give up and move toward a premature and unnecessary dependence upon others. They underestimate their mental skills and avoid continued intellectual stimulation. A low-grade pessimism sinks into their lives.

How do you avoid the crisis of stagnation and dependency? The survivors are those who don't give up. They keep themselves mentally active and involved with people. They also continue to exercise. No matter what their age, exercise is one of the best ways to avoid dependency. The survivors look for ways to continue to grow.[16]

Patrick Morley, in his excellent book *Two-Part Harmony*, shares this about older age:

Once I was invited to preach the Father's Day sermon at a particular church. When I arrived I was taken aback by how few men appeared to be of fathering age.

I asked the youth pastor, "What percentage of the congregation would you estimate to be elderly (over sixty-five)?"

"Seventy percent," he immediately responded.

"And of those, what percentage would you say are lonely?" I further inquired.

"All of them."

Recently a retired man told me, "The notion that when you retire your financial needs will go down is a myth. The trouble is that you build yourself into a certain lifestyle. It's not that easy to just up and change everything."

"How much money is enough, then, to retire?" I asked.

"You can never have too much retirement income," came his reply.

There are two great problems in retirement: *loneliness* and *money.*

As a general rule, the quality of our relationships in retirement will mirror the quality of our relationships today. Loneliness is a choice, one that we make years before we retire—a decision we are making right now. True, some people wouldn't be lonely even if they retired to the South Pole and talked to penguins all day. For most of us, though, the decisions we make right now determine whether we will be lonely in retirement.

We can avoid loneliness in retirement by sound planning and making some investments in other people's lives. The Bible proclaims that we reap what we sow.[17]

Charles Handy, writing for *Modern Maturity,* suggests that we drop the word *retirement* and develop a new attitude and name for this period of our lives, such as "The Third Age of Living." By doing this we acknowledge that a full-time job is just one part of life's journey. The answer to job loss or burnout is a change to a new way of thinking. He calls it a "portfolio" way of thinking. It's full of possibilities.[18]

How to Survive Change

Where do we go from here? What can we learn from those who seem to cope better with the predictable changes of life as well as some of the sudden ones?

People who make positive transitions are those who face life and prepare in advance. They are also able to adjust and sort out which crisis needs to be handled first. For example, one man faced the crisis of his wife being seriously ill in the hospital. Then a major crisis threatened his business. Instead of attempting to juggle both and deal with them as problems of equal weight, he decided that his wife's recovery was most important and nothing else was going to deter him from helping her. Thus, in his own mind the business crisis receded in importance. The second crisis did not add as much to his level of stress as you might expect. By making the decision he did, he was able to stay in control. When we feel as though we are in control, we handle life better.

If you're facing a transition or are in the midst of one, here are some suggestions to help you cope:

1. Look at the stage of life you are leaving. Are you fighting change in any way? What is there that you don't want to give up or change? What makes you uncomfortable with the new role? What would make you more comfortable? Find someone with whom you can discuss your answers to these questions.

2. Seek the advice of someone you respect, whose insights will help you, if you are having difficulty making a decision regarding a change or about determining what plan to follow.

3. Make a specific list of what is involved in making this change in your life. Look for the information through reading and asking others about their experiences.

4. Spend time reading the Psalms. Many of them reflect the struggles of humanity yet give comfort and assurance that God is merciful toward us.

5. Identify specifically what you need to do to help you feel more in control of the situation. And remember that being in control does not mean that you have all of the answers or that you know the outcome or when the situation will be resolved. Being in control means that you've given yourself permission not to have all the answers. You've told yourself that you can handle the uncertainty.

Being in control means that you've allowed Jesus Christ to come and stand with you in this time of uncertainty. His presence gives you the stability and control you need.

Christ's strength is what all of us need to get through this life, for Christ has told us, "My grace is sufficient for you: for My strength is made perfect in weakness" (2 Cor 12:9, NKJV).[19]

APPENDIX

— ◆ —

Moving toward Recovery

At some point it's important to be able to evaluate where you are in your grief process. Dr. Therese Rando, who has made an outstanding contribution to the study of grief and recovery, suggests that we should evaluate recovery by observing changes in ourselves, in our relationship with what we have lost and in our relationships with the world and other people.[1] It often helps to go through this evaluation with a person who can assist you with an objective viewpoint.

As you read and answer the following evaluation statements, your conclusions may help you to decide where you are in your recovery.

On a scale of 0-10 (0 meaning "not at all" and 10 meaning "total recovery in that area"), rate yourself in response to each question. This evaluation is geared toward the loss of a person, but it can be adapted to other losses as well.

Changes in Myself because of My Loss

I have returned to my normal levels of functioning in most areas of my life.

0———————————5———————————10

My overall symptoms of grief have declined.

0———————————5———————————10

My feelings do not overwhelm me when I think about my loss or when someone mentions it.

0————————————5————————————10

Most of the time I feel all right about myself.

0————————————5————————————10

I enjoy myself and what I experience without feeling guilty.

0————————————5————————————10

My anger has diminished, and when it occurs, I handle it appropriately.

0————————————5————————————10

I don't avoid thinking about things that could be or are painful.

0————————————5————————————10

My hurt has diminished and I understand it.

0————————————5————————————10

I can think of positive things.

0————————————5————————————10

I have completed what I need to do about my loss.

0————————————5————————————10

My pain does not dominate my thoughts or my life.

0————————————5————————————10

I can handle special days or dates without feeling totally overwhelmed by memories.

0————————————5————————————10

I have handled the secondary losses that accompanied my major loss.

0————————5————————10

I can remember the loss on occasion without pain and without crying.

0————————5————————10

There is meaning and significance to my life.

0————————5————————10

I am able to ask the question How? rather than Why? at this time.

0————————5————————10

I see hope and purpose in life, in spite of my loss.

0————————5————————10

I have energy and can feel relaxed during the day.

0————————5————————10

I no longer fight the fact that the loss has occurred. I have accepted it.

0————————5————————10

I am learning to be comfortable with my new identity and in being without what I lost.

0————————5————————10

I understand that my feelings over the loss will return periodically, and I can understand and accept that.

0————————5————————10

I understand what grief means and have a greater appreciation for it.

0————————5————————10

Changes in My Relationship with the Person I Lost

I remember our relationship realistically with positive and negative memories.

0————————————5————————————10

The relationship I have with the person I lost is healthy and appropriate.

0————————————5————————————10

I feel all right about not thinking about the loss for a time. I don't feel as though I am betraying the one I lost.

0————————————5————————————10

I have a new relationship with the person I have "lost." I know appropriate ways of keeping the person "alive."

0————————————5————————————10

I no longer go on a search for my loved one.

0————————————5————————————10

I don't feel compelled to hang on to the pain.

0————————————5————————————10

The ways I keep memories of my loved one alive are healthy and acceptable.

0————————————5————————————10

I can think about things in life other than what I lost.

0————————————5————————————10

My life has meaning even though this person is gone.

0————————————5————————————10

Changes I Have Made in Adjusting to My New World

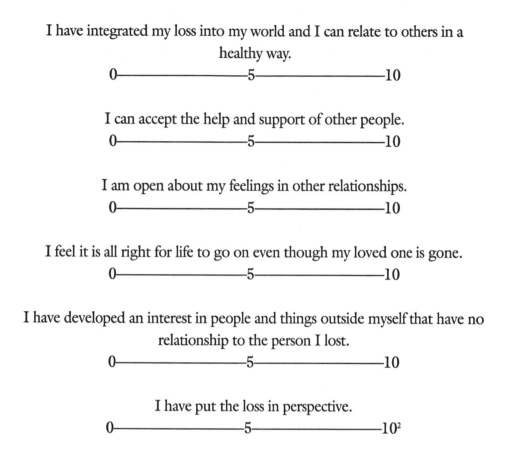

I have integrated my loss into my world and I can relate to others in a
healthy way.

0—————————5—————————10

I can accept the help and support of other people.

0—————————5—————————10

I am open about my feelings in other relationships.

0—————————5—————————10

I feel it is all right for life to go on even though my loved one is gone.

0—————————5—————————10

I have developed an interest in people and things outside myself that have no
relationship to the person I lost.

0—————————5—————————10

I have put the loss in perspective.

0—————————5—————————10²

Grief recovery is a back-and-forth process. One of the better ways to identify your progress is through a personal journal. Writing down your thoughts
will give you proof that you are making progress even though your feelings
say otherwise. Your journal is your own private property and is not for anyone else to read. It is an expression of what you are feeling and your recovery
climb. It can be written in any style—simple statements, poems or prayers
that reflect your journey. The authors of the *Grief Adjustment Guide* offer
some helpful suggestions for keeping a journal.

1. You may find it helpful to make time every day to write at least a short paragraph in your journal. At the end of a week, review what you have written to see small steps of progress toward grief recovery. Writing at least a line or two every day is the most effective way to keep a journal.

2. Some people write in their journals a few times each week, reviewing the entries at the end of the week and at the end of each month. If you have trouble getting started, look over the following list of suggested beginnings. Find one that fits what you are feeling or need to express and use it to "jump start" your writing for that day:

   1. My biggest struggle right now is …
   2. The thing that really gets me down is …
   3. The worst thing about my loss is …
   4. When I feel lonely …
   5. The thing I most fear is …
   6. The most important thing I've learned is …
   7. The thing that keeps me from moving on is …
   8. I seem to cry most when …
   9. I dreamed last night …
   10. I heard a song that reminded me of …
   11. A new person I've come to appreciate is …
   12. I get angry when …
   13. Part of the past that keeps haunting me is …
   14. What I've learned from the past is …
   15. Guilt feelings seem to come most when …
   16. The experiences I miss the most are …
   17. New experiences I enjoy the most are …
   18. The changes I least and most like are …
   19. My feelings sometimes confuse me because …
   20. I smelled or saw something today that reminded me of …
   21. A new hope I found today is …
   22. New strengths I've developed since my loss are …

23. I feel close to God today because ...
24. I am angry at God today because ...
25. For me to find and have balance, I ...
26. I got a call or letter from a friend today that ...
27. My friend,____, had a loss today, and I ... [3]

If one of these doesn't fit, then write about what you are feeling. You could start with just one word—*misery, longing, hope* or whatever—and then describe that feeling with phrases or sentences. If you need to, cry as you write, but keep writing until there is nothing more to say about that feeling.

Your journal is yours to say and feel what is in your heart and mind. It is your way of crystallizing the feelings of loss. Dealing with your feelings one at a time in a written, tangible form is a good way to "own" those feelings and respond to them in an organized way. Grief is a whole tangle of feelings, and writing them down is a great way to isolate and adjust to each one.

Monitor what you write. When you begin to see yourself writing more about what is happening *today* and less about the one you have lost, you'll know that healing and adjustment are indeed taking place, though it may seem painfully slow. Look for signs of progress.

It is *your* journal; use it for your own benefit.[4]

Perhaps the chart on the next page will assist you in your journey of recovery. Use it with the accompanying evaluation questions.

1. Cross out the stages you have already experienced.

2. List ways you have freed yourself from being "stuck" in one phase.

3. Make some statements to yourself about your own patterns of handling loss experiences. (Examples: "I turn inward instead of outward." "I internalize my anger.")

4. List the strengths you now have because of the grief you have experienced. (Examples: "I'm a survivor!" "I've learned empathy for others.")

5. What are some ways you can use these new strengths to help others?[5]

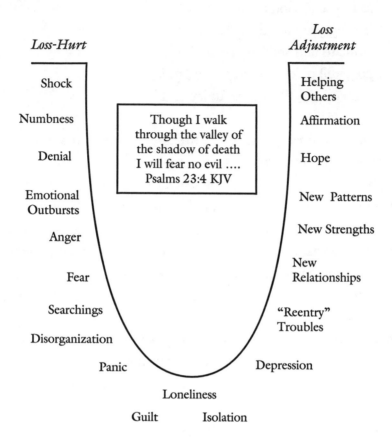

Loss-Hurt

Loss Adjustment

Shock

Numbness

Denial

Emotional Outbursts

Anger

Fear

Searchings

Disorganization

Panic

Helping Others

Affirmation

Hope

New Patterns

New Strengths

New Relationships

"Reentry" Troubles

Depression

Loneliness

Guilt   Isolation

Though I walk through the valley of the shadow of death I will fear no evil ....
Psalms 23:4 KJV

NOTES

— ◆ —

Chapter One

1. Dave Dravecky with Tim Stafford, *Comeback* (Grand Rapids, Mich.: Zondervan, 1990), 16, adapted.
2. Gerald L. Sittser, *A Grace Disguised* (Grand Rapids, Mich.: Zondervan, 1996), 17-18.
3. Langston Hughes, as quoted in Ann Kaiser Stearns, *Living Through Personal Crisis* (Chicago: Thomas Moore, 1984), 25.
4. Marilyn Willett Heavelin, *When Your Dreams Die* (San Bernardino, Calif.: Here's Life, 1990), 30-31.

Two

1. Max Lucado, *In the Eye of the Storm* (Dallas: Word, 1991), 105-6.
2. Lewis Smedes, *How Can It Be All Right when Everything Is All Wrong?* (San Francisco: Harper & Row, 1982), 55-56.
3. Charles Swindoll, *Growing Strong in the Seasons of Life* (Portland, Ore.: Multnomah, 1983), 274-75.
4. Alexander Solzhenitsyn, as quoted in Barry Johnson, *Choosing Hope* (Nashville: Abingdon, 1988), 178.
5. Johnson, 178.
6. Sittser, 62-63.

Three

1. Ann Kaiser Sterns, *Coming Back,* (New York: Random House, 1988), 85-86
2. Gordon MacDonald, as quoted in Gary J. Oliver, *How to Get It Right after You've Gotten It Wrong* (Wheaton, Ill.: Victor, 1995), 48.
3. Gordon MacDonald, as quoted in Oliver, 48.
4. Aaron Lazare et al., "The Walk-In Patient as a 'Customer': A Key Dimension in Evaluation and Treatment," *American Journal of Orthopsychiatry,* 42, 1979), 872-83.
5. Lucado, 193-94, adapted.
6. Frederick Buechner, *Peculiar Treasures: A Biblical Who's Who* (New York: Harper & Row, 1979), 65.
7. Erin Lim, *I Know Just How You Feel: Avoid the Clichés of Grief* (Gary, Ind.: Publishers Mark, 1986), XII, XIII.
8. William Pruitt, *Run from the Pale Pony* (Grand Rapids, Mich.: Baker, 1976), 9-10.

Four

1. Information has been adapted from the following articles: "New Hope, New Dreams" by Roger Rosen Platt, *Time* August 26, 1996 v 148, N10, pg. 40 (13); "Fighting to Fund an Absolute Necessity" by Kendall Hamilton, *Newsweek* July 1, 1996, v. 128, N1, pg. 56 (1); "We Draw Strength from Each Other" by Liz Smith, *Good Housekeeping* June 1996, v. 322, N6, pg. 86 (5).
2. Carol St. Audacher, *Beyond Grief* (Oakland, Calif.: New Harbinger, 1987), 10-31, adapted.
3. Earl A. Grolman, *Living when a Loved One Has Died* (Boston: Beacon, 1987), 39-41.
4. Shirley Inrau, "Learning with a Dying Mother," *Confident Living,* December 1987, 20-22. Used by permission of the author.
5. Maggie Scarf, *Unfinished Business: Pressure Points in the Lives of Women* (New York: Doubleday, 1985), 86, 87.

6. Richard R. Berg and Christine McGarlney, *Depression and the Integrated Life* (New York: Alba House, 1981), 37.

7. David W. Willske, *Gone but Not Lost* (Grand Rapids, Mich.: Baker, 1992), 55, adapted.

Five

1. Therese A. Rando, *Grieving: How to Go on Living when Someone You Love Dies* (Lexington, Mass.: Lexington Books, 1988), 556-57, adapted.

2. Rando, *Grieving*, 44.

3. Therese A. Rando, *Treatment of Complicated Mourning* (Champaigne, Ill.: Research Press, 1983), 512.

4. Glen W. Davidson, *Understanding Mourning* (Minneapolis: Augsburg, 1984), 59. Used by permission.

5. Joyce and Norman Wright, *I'll Love You Forever* (Colorado Springs, Colo.: Focus on the Family, 1993), 69-76, adapted.

6. Wright, 138-50, adapted.

7. Delores Kuenning, *Helping People Through Grief* (Minneapolis: Bethany House, 1987), 227-28, adapted.

8. Ken Gire, *Windows of the Soul* (Grand Rapids, Mich.: Zondervan, 1996), 140.

Six

1. Phillips Brooks, as quoted in Elisabeth Elliot, *Love Has a Price Tag* (Ann Arbor, Mich.: Servant, 1979), 11.

2. Ronald J. Knapp, *Beyond Endurance: When a Child Dies* (New York: Schocken, 1986), 45.

3. Rando, *Grieving*, 181-83, adapted.

4. St. Audacher, 100-101, adapted.

5. Rando, *Grieving*, 169, adapted; Staudacher, 116, adapted.

6. Wright, 41,42,44,45.

7. Rando, *Grieving*, 169, adapted.

8. Knapp, 206.

9. Staudacher, 113, adapted.

10. Knapp, 103, adapted.

11. Knapp, 41.

Seven

1. Donald Meichenbaum, *A Clinical Handbook/Practiced; Therapist Manual for Assessing and Treating Adults with Post Traumatic Stress Disorder (PTSD)* (Waterloo, Ont.: Institute Press, 1994), 23, adapted.

2. Sandra L. Brown, *Counseling Victims of Violence* (Alexandria, Va.: American Association for Counseling and Development, 1991), 9, adapted.

3. Meichenbaum, 510-11, adapted.

4. Aphraodite Matsakis, *I Can't Get over It: A Handbook for Trauma Survivors* (Oakland, Calif.: New Harbinger, 1992), 6-7, adapted.

5. Matsakis, 23-24, adapted.

6. Matsakis, 10-13, adapted.

7. Robert Hicks, *Failure to Scream* (Nashville: Nelson, 1993), 21.

8. C.S. Lewis, *A Grief Observed* (London: Fober & Fober, 1961), 9.

9. Brown, 22-24, adapted.

10. C.S. Lewis, "Relapse," *Poems,* Walter Hooper, ed. (New York: Harcourt Brace Jovanovich, 1964), 103-4.

11. Hicks, 46, adapted.

12. Matsakis, 18-22, adapted.

13. Raymond B. Flammery, Jr., *Post-Traumatic Stress Disorder* (New York: Crossroad, 1992), 36-37, adapted.

14. Matsakis, 134, adapted.

15. Matsakis, 135, 153, adapted.

16. Matsakis, 159, adapted.

17. Matsakis, 160-263, adapted.

18. Matsakis, 236, adapted.

Eight

1. Lloyd J. Ogilvie, *If God Cares, Why Do I Still Have Problems?* (Waco, Tex.: Word, 1985), 18, adapted.

2. Gary Kinnaman, *My Companion through Grief* (Ann Arbor, Mich.: Servant, 1996), 17.

3. Ronald Dunn, *When Heaven Is Silent* (Nashville, Tenn.: Nelson, 1994), 113-14.

4. Dwight Carlson, *When Life Isn't Fair* (Eugene, Ore.: Harvest House, 1989); Harold Kushner, *When Bad Things Happen to Good People* (New York: Avon Books, 1981), 129.

5. C.S. Lewis, *The Problem of Pain* (London: Collins, 1961), 36.

6. Daniel Simundson, *Where Is God in Our Suffering?* (Minneapolis: Augsbury, 1983), 29, quoted in Delores Kuenning, *Helping People through Grief* (Minneapolis: Bethany House, 1987).

7. Smedes, 56.

8. Smedes, 57-59.

9. Sittser, 113-14, adapted.

10. Sittser, 114-15,

11. Philip Yancey, *Where Is God when It Hurts?* (New York: Harper & Row, 1977), 89.

12. Carlson, 38.

13. Carlson, 43.

14. G. Tom Milazzo, *The Protest and the Silence* (Minneapolis: Fortress, 1992), 43.

15. M. Scott Peck, *People of the Lie* (New York: Simon & Schuster, 1983), 41, adapted.

16. Dunn, 62-64, adapted.

17. Don Baker, *Pain's Hidden Purpose* (Portland, Ore.: Multnomah, 1984), 72.

18. Larry Richards, *When It Hurts Too Much to Wait* (Dallas: Word, 1985), 67-68.

19. Yancey, 206-7.

Nine

1. Lucado, 11, adapted.
2. Tim Hansel, *You Gotta Keep Dancin'*, (Colorado Springs, Colo.: David C. Cook, 1985), 90-91.
3. Dr. Joy Joffe, as quoted in Stearns, 62.
4. Dr. Gerald Mann, original source unknown.
5. Hansel, 36-38.
6. Charlie and Lucy Wedemeyer, *Charlie's Victory* (Grand Rapids, Mich.: Zondervan, 1993), 20.
7. Gire, 193-94.
8. Gire, 195.
9. Hicks, 11-12.

Ten

1. Robert Veninga, *A Gift of Hope* (Boston: Little Brown & Co., 1985), 66-70, adapted.
2. Veninga, 71.
3. Wayne Monbleau, *You Don't Find Water on the Mountain Top* (Grand Rapids, Mich.: Revell, 1996), 58, 59.
4. Paul Walker, *How to Keep Your Joy* (Nashville, Tenn.: Thomas Nelson, 1987), 58-59.
5. Hansel, 132-33.
6. Walker, 23.
7. Tom Sullivan, adapted from a speech given to the Million Dollar Round Table Annual Meeting, 1983.
8. Sullivan.
9. Lloyd J. Ogilvie, *God's Best for My Life* (Eugene, Ore.: Harvest House, 1981), 9, used by permission.
10. Walker, 98-99.
11. Swindoll, *The Finishing Touch* (Dallas: Word, 1995), 166-67.
12. Nick Stinnett and John DeFran, *Secrets of Strong Families* (Boston: Little Brown & Co., 1985), 140-41.

13. Stearns, 58-179.

14. Swindoll, *Living on the Ragged Edge,* 110-11.

Eleven

1. Jack Hayford, *Taking Hold of Tomorrow* (Ventura, Calif.: Regal, 1988), 33.

2. Gary Collins, *Family Shock* (Wheaton, Ill.: Tyndale, 1996), 369.

3. Gary Smalley, *Making Love Last Forever* (Dallas: Word, 1996), 72-73.

4. Stephen Covey, *The Seven Habits of Highly Effective People* (New York: Simon & Schuster, 1989), 71-72, adapted.

5. *The Barna Report,* Premiere Issue (Waco, Tex.: Word Ministries Resources, 1996), adapted.

6. R. Scott Sullender, quoted in H. Norman Wright, *Family Is Still a Good Idea* (Ann Arbor, Mich.: Servant, 1992), 248.

7. Charles M. Sell, *Transitions through Adult Life* (Grand Rapids, Mich.: Zondervan, 1985), 161.

8. Gail Sheehy, *New Passages* (New York: Random House, 1995), 4-6, adapted.

9. Swindoll, *Living on the Ragged Edge,* 107-8.

10. Linda Stern, "How to Find a Job," *Modern Maturity* June/July 1993, 25, adapted.

11. Barry Glasner, *Career Crash* (New York: Simon & Schuster, 1995), 34, adapted.

12. Jim Smoke, *Facing Fifty* (Nashville: Nelson, 1994), 127.

13. Sheehy, 65-71, adapted.

14. Glasner, 180-85, adapted.

15. Smoke, 148-49.

16. Sheehy, 427-29, adapted.

17. Patrick Morley, *Two-Part Harmony* (Nashville: Nelson, 1994), 234-35.

18. Charles Handy, "Building Smaller Fires: Keep Life Sizzling-Diversity," *Modern Maturity,* October/November 1991, 35, adapted.

19. Wright, *Secrets of a Lasting Marriage,* 113, adapted.

Appendix

1. Rando, *Grieving,* 281-83, adapted.

2. Rando, *Grieving,* 284-86, adapted.

3. Charlotte Greeson, Mary Hollingsworth, and Michael Washburn, *The Grief Adjustment Guide* (Sisters, Ore.: Questar, 1990), 90, 91.

4. Greeson, Hollingsworth, and Washburn, 90, 91.

5. Greeson, Hollingsworth, and Washburn, 68. and Wright, *Recovering from the Losses of Life,* 115-22, adapted.

ACKNOWLEDGMENTS

— ◆ —

Materials taken from *You Gotta Keep Dancin'* by Tim Hansel, Chariot Victor Publishing, ©1986. Used by permission of Chariot Victor Publishing.

Materials taken from *Depression and the Integrated Life* by Richard R. Berg and Dr. Christine McCartney, ©1981. Used by permission of Alba House.

Materials taken from *Transitions through Adult Life* by Charles M. Sell. ©1985 by Moody Bible Institute. Used by permission of Zondervan Publishing House.

Materials taken from *Family Shock* by Gary R. Collins, ©1995. Used by permission of Tyndale House Publishers, Inc. All rights reserved.

Materials taken from *Unfinished Business* by Maggie Scarf, Bantam/Doubleday Publishing, ©1985. Used by permission of Bantam/Doubleday Publishing.

Materials taken from *The Protest and the Silence* by G. Tom Milazzo, Augsburg Fortress, ©1992. Used by permission of Augsburg Fortress.

Materials taken from *When Life Isn't Fair* by Dwight Carlson, ©1989 by Harvest House Publishers, Eugene, Oregon. Used by permission.

Materials taken from *How to Get It Right After You've Gotten It Wrong* by Gary Oliver, Chariot Victor Publishing, ©1995. Used by permission of Chariot Victor Publishing.